PRAISE FOR *KILL THE NOISE*

"*Kill the Noise* by my friend Rynum send for the Kingdom of Go.......... s is a book about adventurously li.................ming over in your heart, as you bid farewell .... ace an exciting friendventure with the God of hope. Read it. Get one for your friend. And skateboard with Ryan into the colony and outpost of heaven he's creating on earth."

—Ben Courson, founder of Hope Generation, international speaker, pastor, TV and radio personality, and bestselling author of *Optimisfits* and *Flirting with Darkness*

"My friend Ryan Ries has always been very transparent about how his obsession with hard-core drug use and women permeated his former life to levels that would shock even the most seasoned partiers. But the biggest shocker is how God has completely redirected Ryan's passion from party animal to displaying the real and tangible love of Christ to thousands of young people with the Whosoevers' *Kill the Noise* tour!

"*Kill the Noise* isn't just another book. *Kill the Noise* is a life-igniting tool that carries authentic power to guide the most wounded and defeated souls straight into this mystery of Christ within. The last thing the world needs right now is another watered-down religious book! We need raw. We need real. We need authentic. We need to *KILL THE NOISE*."

—Brian "Head" Welch, co-founder of the Grammy Award–winning band Korn, *New York Times* bestselling author of *Save Me From Myself, Stronger,* and *With My Eyes Wide Open,* and co-star of the Showtime movie *Loud Krazy Love*

"I've known Ryan for more than eleven years and will never forget the day I met him with my fiancé (at the time) Oz Fox. With tears in his eyes, he shared his incredible story of how God took his wild, rebellious heart and transformed it into a burning flame of love for God and His people.

"Raw, refreshing, and beautifully, brutally honest. That's the only way I can describe Ryan's radical story of transformation in *Kill the Noise*. This book will captivate you, inspire you, and motivate you to live and learn more about the amazing grace of God and the power of surrender. Like fresh wind from heaven, Ryan's journey is masterfully and honestly written, full of twists and turns into the dark world of addiction and rock and roll. But, ultimately, it finds its way into the bright world of redemption and true liberty of the soul.

"Ryan is the real deal. He went above and beyond on this book… and I just could not put this down…neither will you!"

—Annie Lobert, wife of Oz Fox (Stryper), founder and CEO of Hookers For Jesus and Annie's Pink Chair

"Like John the Baptist before him, Ryan's book is like a voice shouting in the wilderness, 'Clearing the way for the LORD's coming!' Refreshingly raw and vulnerable, this former 'cocaine pirate' has become a prophetic voice for an entire generation the world over!"

—Phil Evans, pastor of Hawkesbury Valley Baptist Church, Australia

"Ryan Ries, though raised by loving parents in a pastor's home, was no choirboy. His rebellion was fueled by the streets and party scene of Los Angeles, California. I've known him as someone with a passion for the lost, and now I know why—he himself *was* lost. In *Kill the Noise*, Ryan is brutally honest about his life experiences, temptations, bad choices (and good), and how he once avoided—even hated—God. His voice is fresh as he describes the antiestablishment Jesus of the New Testament and how he came to surrender to His control. What's more, Ryan shares the secrets he's discovered along the way in his own faith journey and how he's learned to turn both victory and calamity into a testimony. This is an honest account of a radically transformed life."

—Skip Heitzig, pastor of Calvary Church, Albuquerque, New Mexico, and bestselling author of *The Bible from 30,000 Feet*

"It has been an honor and a privilege to know Ryan, and to walk with him side by side on his journey of faith. I met Ryan when he was lost and at his lowest point of life, and I am now watching him become what I truly believe to be a great evangelist of our time. His love for Jesus is convicting, and his childlike faith is contagious. His new book, *Kill the Noise*, is the most honest, sincere, and relatable book I've read in a while, and is guaranteed to capture the heart of anyone who reads it."

—Sonny Sandoval, lead singer of the multiplatinum band P.O.D.

"I have known and loved Ryan since a baby. He had dark days, or should I say dark years, as I did. When his life changed, thousands of lives also ended up changing because of his boldness to tell others about Christ. He wants to talk with you through much love and experience and grief. After thirty-plus years sharing my gift of evangelism with tens of thousands in stadiums, bull rings, and sports arenas, only one name have I heard recently in Mexico that is stirring leaders in a positive way, giving Mexico hope. That name belongs to someone who is like a son to me. That name is Ryan Ries!"

—Dr. Mike MacIntosh, pastor, evangelist, and police and fire chaplain

"What makes Ryan's testimony powerful is that it's relatable. He grew up trying to find himself in the things the world had to offer, struggling with the same vices as myself and everyone else who grows up skateboarding, pushing the boundaries of the law, and listening to counterculture music. He's tasted and seen it all, and it left him empty and broken. But Jesus reached into his life and met him where he was at, radically transforming his life from the inside out. However, in all of this transformation, Ryan still remains down to earth, engaging with the cultures he was saved in, remembering what it's like to be searching for meaning, broken, and in need of a Savior. That's what makes a book like this powerful. You will hear the truth about Jesus from someone who has walked in your shoes."

—Steven Bancarz, YouTuber and speaker, and co-author of
The Second Coming of the New Age

"Reading through the first few pages of Ryan's book reminded me of the real pull and allure of this world. It's become so common now that pulpits around the country don't even warn against the evils of drugs, carnality, and the associated sins of a life in rebellion toward God. Yet, like anyone connected to God, there is a turning point. Tears welled up in my eyes as I thought of how precious the scene was as Ryan asked God to forgive him, in one of his worst moments! God did and filled that young man with His Holy Spirit. Anyone who has spent any time with Ryan knows the power of God's Spirit is evident in his life! He inspires me by his obedience and commitment! Ryan speaks of a living God, not dead religion. Read to the end. You will be stirred toward more love and good works!"

—Ed Taylor, pastor of Calvary Church, Aurora, Colorado

"Ryan Ries is a voice that needs to be heard today, because he understands all too well what it means to 'kill the noise' in his life. He is speaking from a life that once had an ear for the noise of the world, until Jesus brought him to the end of himself and caused the noise of this world to cease. This opened up a whole new world to him and gave him an ear to hear God's voice. This book is a must-read for young and old alike."

—Tony Clark, pastor of Calvary Chapel, Newport News

"Spending ten years of my life in a rock band on tour, I thought I knew what it meant to be a rock star. After reading Ryan Ries's book *Kill the Noise*, I quickly found that I was mistaken. Ryan communicates in modern terminology how Jesus Christ was the first and truest rock star to ever live.

"This book is for the broken. This book is for the marathon runners chasing after a greater high over and over again until it kills them. But most important, this book is for those who hear the words 'church,' 'God,' 'Jesus,' or 'Christianity' and get a bad taste in their mouths.

"We all hate posers. *Kill the Noise* clearly shows that Ryan is not a poser, and, most important, that Jesus was not either. You think you know Christianity? You think you know Jesus? You think you know transformation? Wait until you read this book and allow God to transform you through my friend Ryan Ries's wild story."

—Austin Carlile, former lead singer of Of Mice & Men

"This is an amazing book! Ryan is extremely connected to what is happening in the world today. This book challenges you to have a relationship with God not based on a list of requirements but on a fresh, real, raw, and fearless life in the Spirit.

"I absolutely enjoyed the book from cover to cover. Powerful like dynamite!"

—Jesser Gaona, youth pastor of Semilla Cuernavaca, Mexico

"In his new book, *Kill the Noise*, Ryan Ries writes with passion his personal story of the saving Grace of God. Like a modern David, Ryan has a heart after God. His heart burns with a fire that reminds me of the early Church. God is pouring out His Spirit in these last days just as He promised through the prophet Joel 'for such a time as this.' And now that fire is spreading everywhere he goes. Get ready to be set ablaze!"

—Ray Bentley, author, and pastor of Maranatha Chapel

"I've gotten so tired of image-focused and 'brand-managed' Christian personalities that I won't read or recommend 99 percent of what's out there. Why? Because it's often disingenuous and not really written to help reach lost people or struggling people with major challenges. But Ryan Ries's new book, *Kill the Noise*, made it into that 1 percent list! This book is raw, real, and riveting, and will help anyone who picks it up. It's much needed at this time in history in a way that inspires me to tell everyone about it!"

—Victor Marx, founder and president, All Things Possible Ministries and the Victor Marx Group

"Ryan has had a crazy and amazing life that continues to call him to Jesus. I have always admired how he tells his story in real language easily understood by anyone, especially those stumbling through life looking for purpose and meaning. His story is raw, explicit, and dark—but he keeps the Word of God that saved him woven throughout. I am so thankful for Ryan's honest and compelling voice in our culture, pulling no punches with those who hunger for truth."

—JW Clarke, Billy Graham Evangelistic Association
and Birdhouse Group, Inc.

"In *Kill the Noise*, Ryan Ries transparently details his epic life journey while dishing out constant nuggets of spiritual truth. His story gets your attention, but the spiritual truth penetrates deep into the heart. This book amplifies the impact Ryan already makes through The Whosevers, and can reach those in need of direction."

—John Humphrey, vice president of I Am Second

"When I began to read this book, I thought that it would really help those caught up in drugs, alcohol, and meaningless sex. Halfway through, I thought this will help people who want to find out if God and Christianity are real. Having finished reading, I think this is a book for everyone who wants to live a sold-out life for Christ, whether you are eighteen or eighty-five. It's not too late to be who God has called you to be."

—Sheila Walsh, bestselling author, and co-host of *Life Today*

"Ryan Ries and his new book, *Kill the Noise*, are the real deal. I spent a week reading his book and each day, each chapter, and each page spoke so deeply into my life. It was convicting, truth-filled, and raw. I am looking forward to giving this book to people in my world who I know are struggling with in their walk with Christ, and also to nonbelievers in the modeling industry that I'm a part of. This book is for this generation, it's for the church, it's for the wayward Christian, and it's for those who want to live the life Jesus lived. It's truly a bridge from the messiness of this world to the foot of the cross, for people to find salvation and true transformation. I truly believe that *Kill the Noise* is going to bring a raw voice and raw truth to hearts around the world."

—Christina Boudreau, TED Talk speaker,
plus-size model, and author

"Over the years, I watched my son Ryan pursue a life of emotional, physical, and spiritual destruction. In his book, *Kill the Noise*, you will be blown away, as I have been, to see how the Holy Spirit intercepted him and took control of his life. The Lord has truly anointed Ryan to preach the Gospel. Through his witness, thousands of teens and adults have turned from a life of ruin and received the redemption that is found in Jesus Christ. Be amazed!"

—Dr. Raul Ries, pastor of Calvary Chapel Golden Springs in
Diamond Bar, California, evangelist, radio host, and author

"*Kill the Noise*—after a moment of a silent encounter with God, Ryan's wretched life was renewed. Empowered by the Holy Spirit, he has taken up the baton of the Gospel message and now uniquely proclaims it to the masses. Delve into his book to become a witness of his miraculous deliverance from sin. Be astonished at God's work through him to bring salvation to those who, like him, were lost."

—Sharon Faith Ries, Women's Bible teacher at Calvary Chapel
Golden Springs in Diamond Bar, California, missionary, and author

"As a DJ for a large Christian radio network, I found Ryan's approach to reaching the culture with the Bible absolutely intriguing! I am someone who does not read books often, yet I found this book so captivating that I couldn't put it down! His voice of reason using

Scripture is difficult to find today in the Christian scene. *Kill the Noise* is essential for any Christian who wants to be fired up!"

—AJ Kestler, director and DJ, Effect Radio Network

"Ryan Ries's new book, *Kill the Noise*, is gripping and Spirit-filled! It's solid biblically, yet easy to understand for anyone. I respect how Ries wasn't concerned about touching on subjects that are considered taboo by many of today's churches. From his testimony to discipleship, this book was thought-provoking, and left me encouraged and wanting more!"

—Mike Kestler, founder and radio host of
To Every Man an Answer, CSN International

"When the Amalakites attacked Israel in the wilderness, God instructed Moses to go to the top of a mountain and raise the staff of God. As long as the staff was held in the air God would help the Israelites take ground, but when the staff was lowered the Israelites lost ground. One of the lessons I believe God is trying to teach us through this story is the importance of partnership with Him; He will always do his part, so we have to do ours. I must admit, as a Christian businessman, trusting that God will do his part is sometimes a struggle for me. In Ryan's amazing book he beautifully displays the importance of A-type personalities like me doing our part, then resting in the fact that He will do His. If you're struggling with partnering with God in any aspect of your life, I want to encourage you to not only read this book but apply the lessons too!"

—Remi Adeleke, bestselling author, former Navy SEAL, filmmaker,
consultant, and author of *Transformed*

"No one is beyond Christ's redemption! Thank you, Ryan, for sharing your story of transformation from the inside out by the indwelling power of the Holy Spirit. Hope will spring forth, and be within reach, for all the Whosoevers, as they read your story. May God continue to use you to inspire and reach your generation with the gospel of Jesus Christ."

—Ron Brown, executive director of Teen Challenge Southern California

"*Kill The Noise* will absolutely relate to anyone who reads it, whether young or old, Christian or not. Ryan will make you both laugh and cry, encouraging you and also challenging you. I don't know of any other voice to society like Ryan's. He's as raw and real as it gets, telling his story and explaining the truths of Christianity in a bold and realistic light, with a refreshing down-to-earth style that brings back the power of the legit and epic Gospel of Jesus at work today, just like we see in the book of Acts. It was written and published during the Coronavirus pandemic, and I believe God will use this book to bring prophetic purification to the church at exactly the time we need it. America needs Christians who keep it real, are full of zeal, and aren't posers. I will be buying copies for my whole youth group."

—Jairus Hodges, founder and pastor of ZEAL Student Ministries

KILL
THE
NOISE

Finding Meaning above
the Madness

RYAN RIES

WORTHY
PUBLISHING
New York • Nashville

Worthy Books
Hachette Book Group
1290 Avenue of the Americas, New York, NY 10104
worthypublishing.com
twitter.com/WorthyPub

First Edition: May 2021

Worthy is a division of Hachette Book Group, Inc. The Worthy name and logo are trademarks of Hachette Book Group, Inc.

The publisher is not responsible for websites (or their content) that are not owned by the publisher.

The Hachette Speakers Bureau provides a wide range of authors for speaking events. To find out more, go to www.hachettespeakersbureau.com or call (866) 376-6591.

Library of Congress Cataloging-in-Publication Data
Names: Ries, Ryan, author.
Title: Kill the noise : finding meaning above the madness / Ryan Ries.
Description: First edition. | New York : Worthy Books, 2021. | Summary: "It doesn't matter who you are or what you've done, God wants a relationship with you. When we turn to the Lord, He is there waiting to forgive us and give us a purpose for our lives. Unfortunately, teens and adults are surrounded by so much noise from social media, the entertainment industry, drugs, pornography, the occult, bullying, and social expectations that it is nearly impossible to hear the truth of a God who will take them as they are. This book is written to help this generation kill that noise, so that teens and adults can hear the voice of God telling them they are loved, they are wanted, and they are His. Ryan Ries is living proof of this truth. Growing up in Los Angeles, California as the son of a mega-church pastor, but surrounded by the music, skate, and snowboard industries, Ryan felt a tug-of-war between the church and the world. It was in the skate and music culture that he found his passion and his identity. So he walked away from God and dove head first into the world, losing his way in alcohol, drugs, and sex, which lead to anxiety, brokenness, and emptiness. Kill the Noise is his story about finding God in the messiness of life, even though it seemed impossible, and will help readers find Him too"— Provided by publisher.
Identifiers: LCCN 2020054041 | ISBN 9781546017448 (trade paperback) | ISBN 9781546017431 (ebook)
Subjects: LCSH: Ries, Ryan. | Christian biography—United States. | Children of clergy—United States--Biography. | Addicts—United States—Biography. | Evangelists—United States—Biography. | Young adults--Religious life. | Rave culture—California—Los Angeles. | Sex addiction—United States. | Drug addiction—United States.
Classification: LCC BR1725.R57185 A3 2021 | DDC 277.94/94092 [B]—dc23
LC record available at https://lccn.loc.gov/2020054041

ISBNs: 978-1-5460-1744-8 (trade pbk.), 978-1-5460-1743-1 (ebook)

Printed in the United States of America
LSC-C
PRINTING 1, 2021

This book is dedicated to my beautiful wife, Crystal,
who has stood with me through the mountaintop experiences
and the storms, to my three beautiful triplet daughters
and my amazing son, and to my parents Raul and Sharon Ries.

"The eyes of the Lord search the whole earth in order to
strengthen those whose hearts are fully committed to him."

2 Chronicles 16:9

CONTENTS

CHAPTER 1

Let the Good Times Roll

It was the summer of 1993—I was eighteen years old and ready for anything. I pulled my Honda Civic, nicknamed The UFO, up to a 7-Eleven, and my buddy Gerardo jumped out of the front seat. He dropped a quarter into a pay phone, punched in some numbers, and was connected with the underground hotline. The voice on the other end gave him some directions, then disconnected. Gerardo ran back to the car and dropped into the front seat. Turning to me, then toward our three friends who were sardined in the back, he said with a grin, "It's on. We're set."

I knew that look. I had seen it before. This was going to be epic. During our last trip up to San Francisco, Gerardo had introduced us to techno music. Going to Haight-Ashbury, he bought us a Ron D Core mixtape. We listened to that cassette for eight hours on our way back down to LA, psyched on what we heard. Then, earlier this week, Gerardo had told us that Insomniac was putting on a rave in LA. The rave scene was still young and he had been to a few. He told us they were insane and said we had to get ourselves to one. That's what was going down tonight.

Okay, Gerardo, it's on! Let's do this, G! I punched the pedal to the metal and we were out.

We drove through LA late at night—our windows were up, we were taking bong rips and hot boxing the car, and we were getting warmed up, bumping that same techno mixtape. We had been smoking weed all day, of course, and now we each dropped some hits of LSD. It took an hour for the acid to kick in full effect, so we were trying to time it just right for showing up to the party. As we weaved through the cars, we were hoping for no LA traffic jams. God forbid we end up out on the 101, jammed into The UFO, peaking on LSD.

Soon we were off the freeways and driving the streets, trying to read the signs in the midnight dark. We were in a seriously sketchy area just outside downtown. It was the last place a group of high seventeen- and eighteen-year-olds should have been. But we were young and stupid and absolutely invincible. Finally, we crossed some railroad tracks and spotted the correct warehouse just off of Santa Fe. Parking next to the tracks, we got out and started toward the door.

Well before we reached the building, we could feel the heavy throbbing bass—*whoom, whoom, whoom, whoom.* Gerardo looked at us and grinned again. We had timed the LSD just right.

The place was a run-down warehouse—old, dirty, industrial. The dude throwing the party took my five bucks and I walked in. Techno was blasting out of a wall of speakers stacked one on top of the other. Dozens of ravers climbed the speakers and were getting their rave on, some wearing Cat in the Hat hats, baggy rave gear, Day-Glo beads, and Mickey Mouse gloves. This mass of partiers was swarming the big black speaker boxes like ants attacking a piece of candy. This wasn't like any concert I'd ever been to. Everyone wanted to be as close as possible—some with their heads right up against the speakers. They didn't want to just hear the music; they wanted to feel every beat.

I stood there trying to wrap my mind around what I was watching. It wasn't easy, because I was peaking on LSD, and I only had a loose grip on reality. I can't remember a lot about the night, but I know that by the time I left I was hooked. When's the next one? Count me in!

When we finally walked outside, someone yelled, "Look, all the cars got broken into!" My heart dropped. I looked up and saw that all the car windows up and down the street were shattered. Not only that, but it looked like someone had taken a baseball bat to all the car bodies, too. They were totaled. But when we got closer, we realized that nothing had actually happened to them. We had been hallucinating from the high of the LSD. We looked at each other and started laughing.

This was my introduction to the LA underground rave scene and it was sick! Sometimes I wonder how I survived it—how can I possibly still be alive? And I'm not talking just that event, but all the years of partying. I have way too many friends who didn't make it. It wasn't the raves that took them down. The raves were just a new place to do what we had already been doing up in the hills around the city. What took my friends down were the drugs. The acid, ecstasy, meth, booze, and cocaine— taking them individually or combining them, trying to take the high to the next level. For some the ride just got too wild.

One guy I knew was up three days on meth. Then he took a hit of LSD, bad tripped, and jumped off a cliff. The cops made me identify his body. That was my junior year in high school. Another guy took LSD, beat up his dad, and took a dive out of a second-story window before getting arrested by the cops and put in the hospital. Years down the road, I was almost a casualty like them. But God's grace saved me from an early grave and gave me hope and peace and purpose.

That rave was the first of many nights spent in grimy ware- houses. Once I went the first time, I was all in. I kept going back. It was unique, it was underground, and it was illegal. That was my vibe. It was LA underground, and I couldn't get enough.

––––––––––––

I grew up like a lot of other Southern California kids. My family lived in La Verne, right next to San Dimas, where they filmed the famous *Bill & Ted's Excellent Adventure*. We had a condo at the beach in San Clemente, where we'd spend a lot of weekends surfing and skateboarding. Home life was great. My parents loved each other and they loved my brothers and me. My dad pastored a Calvary Chapel megachurch. In every family there are challenges—there are no families that are perfect. But mine was about as close as you could get to ideal.

In the late '80s, the LA underground was hugely creative, as it always is, and thoroughly antiestablishment. The music was in-your-face and raw. Groups like Minor Threat, Black Flag, Suicidal Tendencies, and Social Distortion were playing the clubs. The telephone poles lining Melrose Avenue were covered with concert fliers showing angry cartoonish figures and creative lettering. Album covers were either graphically simple or intricately designed. It was a rad time to be growing up.

I was the youngest of three. My two older brothers, Raul Jr. and Shane, were deep in the skinhead, mod, and punk movements of the time. My brother Shane was in a thrashing power pop band called The Key that played gigs on the LA circuit. I remember one day Shane brought home his new girlfriend. He introduced her: "Hey, this is Gwen Stefani." Later on, I found out her band, No Doubt, was opening for The Key. It seemed like every day there was something new to see or to experience. I was a skater and a surfer, and I was surrounded by the music scene and the counterculture. Punks, mods, skinheads, and rude boys were always coming in and out of the house. A bully picked on me one day, so I had some skinheads on their Vespas pick me up from middle school. He never bothered me again. I loved the "do what you want" rebel mentality. Break the rules? Yes, please! Middle finger in the air like you just don't care! Like Eminem says, that attitude is who I became, and it got worse the older I got. I didn't want to hurt anyone; I just didn't want people telling me what I could and couldn't do—and I mean no one.

My brothers weren't into the drug scene, but drugs and alcohol were a big part of the culture then, just as they are now. Sex, drugs, and rock 'n' roll. They were all around me, and it was just a matter of time before I got sucked in. I didn't want to read about it or hear about it; I wanted to experience it firsthand. So, I dove in headfirst. Then in high school I heard the Beastie Boys, and I realized that finally I had found a band that I could identify with—their music and their lifestyle. They were all about getting drunk, smoking weed, hooking up with chicks, and having a good time.

That's when I started holding my own parties. We'd go from house to house to do them like you do in high school—if anyone had parents that were down for the cause, me and the AWOL (absent without leave) crew would be there. I'd work with a friend on some artwork, have a flier campaign, then work with some more friends to get some production going for the event—sort of a pre-version of the work that I do now—and people would show up by the carloads. Everyone knew an AWOL party was going to be epic. Backyard ragers with black lights, DJs, and nitrous tanks. Music was blasting and people were having a good ol' time. We'd be smoking weed, doing mushrooms, and passing out nitrous balloons. That and the LSD were what opened the door to the psychedelic realm that led me into classic rock—Hendrix, the Doors, the Beatles, and the Grateful Dead.

Those wild nights were why it was so easy for me to slip into the rave movement—I was already throwing crazy parties. Partying became my life—you know, having a good time. Get high, get drunk, and go nuts with the crew! I got the name Rock 'n' Roll Ryan when I was out on tour with UK drum and bass DJs Roni Size, DJ Krust, and DJ Die. To my close friends, I was Wild Out Ries or Ice. My brothers called me The Wild Beast.

———————

As far back as I can remember, I always had a craving for the things the world offers. The Bible talks about them as "the lust of the flesh, the lust of the eyes, and the pride of life" (1 John 2:16 NKJV). The writer of that verse, the disciple John, goes on to make it clear that those are desires that are not of God the Father but of the enemy, the devil. That devil, Satan, is using these body appetites to get into today's youth and seriously mess them up.

The lust attack started for me back in first grade. I was walking behind my school one day and discovered a duffel full of porn magazines. It was hard-core XXX stuff. I had no real understanding of what was taking place in the pictures I was looking at—how could I at that age? Even as I turned from one page to the next, I knew that I should stop because what I was looking at was wrong. If I close my eyes, I can still see some of those pictures today, more than thirty years later. That's the effect of pornography—once it's seared into your mind, there's no getting rid of it. Your brain is like a computer hard drive. Everything you look at gets saved, and there's no delete button. It gets filed deep in your memory bank until it pops back up at the worst times. You'll be sitting in church or driving your car with your kids or on a date night with your spouse and suddenly it's there, playing on the big screen in your brain. Porn messes with relationships. It messes with marriages. It affects the brain and can even lead to impotency.[1] Research shows that long-term porn use alters the same areas of the brain as heroin addiction.[2] Seriously, put the book down and google "your brain on porn and heroin." Wow, right? This is a growing problem in the US and many other areas of the world.

About five years after that first discovery, I walked into my friend's house and his brother had some XXX hard-core porn showing on the TV. Watching that video finally helped me to understand what had been going on in the magazine pictures. Those images changed the way I thought of women. Later in life, I began viewing females as objects—as something to be used for my own pleasure just like in the porn I watched. What I saw opened my mind up to sexual issues that my preteen self wasn't equipped to process. It started the fires of lust, sex, and porn that plagued me in years to come.

There were weird sensations growing inside of me as I watched the screen at my friend's house. Some were physical, but others were spiritual. Looking back now, I believe these other feelings were the grieving of the Holy Spirit. It was His conviction in my heart. The Spirit's sadness came from my loss of innocence. He felt pain because He knew even back then how that moment was going to affect me in the future. That grieving takes place many times every day as more and more kids are exposed to these kinds of images. It used to be difficult for most kids to get their hands on pornography. But now it's only a couple of button pushes away on every smartphone that's in the pocket of kids and adults across America.

And it's not just here in the US. When I was on recent speaking tours down in Mexico and Colombia, I saw that every kid had a cell phone. The same is true all around the world. A 2017 statistic showed that the average age that kids are first exposed to pornography is thirteen, with some as young as five. Nearly half (43.5 percent) of those first exposures were accidental.[3] Whether kids go looking for pornography or they accidentally stumble across it on an internet search, or whether it pops up on YouTube or Instagram, or it's direct messaged to them, innocence is being stolen each and every day.

I was in high school when I was first introduced to cocaine. I had been smoking weed all day when my buddy Dusty got a page to head over to Sheldon's house to go blaze. We parked and walked into the garage where my friend's older brother was rolling cocoa puffs—marijuana joints with cocaine sprinkled in. We sat in a circle and it got passed to me. I hit it hard with a few big rips. After we smoked, I walked out to my car and just sat there thinking, "Dude! I'm so high right now!" That first try opened my eyes to a whole new world. From that point on, cocaine became my friend.

Of course, my parents quickly figured out what was going on. They found my weed stashes and my marijuana plant. Once, they even discovered a hundred hits of liquid LSD in my room. They did all they could to get me help, but I wasn't having it. I was living my life the way I wanted to live it. It became a big source of conflict in our home, much as it is for every other middle school, high school, and college-age kid who is going through the same thing. I was trying to get everything past my parents, while they were trying to shut it all down.

Every day I would wake and bake. As soon as I got up, I'd hit the bong. For the rest of the day I'd keep smoking weed, maybe pick up a forty ounce, then crash out at night. A lot of our crew began getting kicked out of school, because we were getting into so much trouble. My friend Sean McKeehan got expelled for throwing rocks at the teachers' cars and doing thousands of dollars' worth of damage. The rest of us were living out our own stupid reasons for getting asked to leave the school for good. I got sent to continuation school. After a few months there, I just said forget it. I sucked at school anyway. If I was going to do something with my life, it certainly wasn't going to happen for me in an "institutional learning environment." Time passed. Each day was like the day before—the only variations came with the people, the locations, and just how wasted we got.

The only part of my life that was strong enough to pull me away from the drugs was my passion to create and produce events. Again, my love for this began back when I was putting together those high school parties. Just like back then, my mind was always thinking of ideas and concepts and how I could make the experiences bigger and better. I needed to find outlets for all this passion and creative energy that was pouring through me. I started putting on shows and club events around this time, and I started getting paid. That's when it all came together. I saw that I could actually make money producing these events. Pulling in cash while I was doing rad events and hanging out with people and having fun? Dude, that's what's up!

That's when I also realized that the drugs were majorly interfering with my ability to build a business off my ideas. My life was out of control because of all the substances I was dumping into my system. So, I stopped the drugs. I decided I didn't want that life anymore. People ask me how I was able to just stop the drugs cold turkey. Three things—first, I have ADD and I am very passionate about whatever I throw myself into. So, when I decided to pursue this ideas-and-event-producing career, I went full speed, cutting out anything that was going to get in the way.

Second, I was still young and living in my parents' house, which sucked. This was my ticket out. Third, I significantly increased my alcohol consumption. This allowed me to focus hard on my work, then wind down with a six-pack of beer or more at the end of the day. While this is in no way a path to sobriety that I would recommend, it worked for me at the time.

And obviously, it made a huge difference. Rather than wasting time partying and getting nothing out of it, I started producing parties and doing graphic design projects for a record label. Don't get me wrong—I was still drinking way more than I should. But at least my transition from the rave scene to the bar scene helped to keep me a little more grounded on planet Earth.

That's when I fell in love with the wrong girl. I met her in a dive bar, and before I knew it, we had this totally sex-based relationship going on. And that's really all it was about at first. I wasn't even that into her in the beginning. But once you start having sex all the time, it's hard to break away. It's the body appetites I was telling you about—the raging lust of the flesh living itself out.

That's the big reason for the guidelines and boundaries about sex in the Bible. It isn't because God wants to be a creeper lurking around our bedrooms. Hebrews 13:4 says, "Give honor to marriage, and remain faithful to one another in marriage. God will surely judge people who are immoral and those who commit adultery." It's not that He wants to keep us from having any fun. It's exactly the opposite. God wants you to have tons of fun in the bedroom, but it's got to be with your spouse. That's how He made us. We were created so that sex is more than just a physical act. There's an emotional and spiritual side to it, too. So, He created guidelines for keeping it inside of marriage because He knew how sleeping around could seriously confuse our emotions and lead to all sorts of bad situations, messed-up relationships, and STDs. It can even lead to abortions and all the screwed-up emotions and aftereffects that come with that. Sadly, abortion is exactly where this girl and I ended up.

One day, she showed up at my work bawling. She told me that she just got back from aborting our baby at the clinic. This was the first time I even knew she was pregnant. Now she's telling me she aborted our kid? I was in shock. It was like a bomb had been dropped on me. But she was near hysterical, so I wrapped her up in my arms. My own feelings about what had just happened got shoved to the side. Instead, the compassionate side of me came out. People don't often think about how badly getting an abortion messes girls up. It took her a long time to work through what she had done. It was during this time of my emotional shock and her being a wreck that we ended up falling in love.

Then I got her pregnant again. Here was our chance to do it right this time. We stopped the partying, and she took her prenatal care seriously. At one appointment early on, we got the news that the egg had split into twins. But before we had a chance to celebrate, the doctor told us that the second baby had died. He called it vanishing twin syndrome. That news sucked.

But we still had the one baby. We were living clean—doing the best we could for this new life we were bringing into the world. I was determined to be the father this child needed, not a wastoid or a deadbeat. I started having all these fantasies about what it was going to be like being a dad. A short time later, though, she called me and told me that she was too young to be a mom and she was going to abort the baby. She said she still wanted to be with me, but I told her that if she aborted our baby, I would be gone. She did it anyway.

Emptiness. Then rage.

Two pregnancies—three babies gone. All the hope that I had for life turning around was crushed. Then, as one more knife to the back, I found out she was cheating on me. She had already cheated on me before, in between the abortions, but I had decided then that I was going to stick around and try to make it work. Forget that now. We were done.

Some may say, "Dude, what did you expect?" I don't know. I expected something different—something better. Maybe some grace and mercy from God and a chance at both of us turning our lives around and becoming a family. People can change, right? Maybe I was naïve. Maybe I had crazy, unrealistic expectations. All I know is that when it all fell apart, I fell apart with it.

Rather than considering the possibility that my own bad choices may have led to my current situation, I decided the blame belonged to God. Even though I didn't have a relationship with Him, I still accused Him of destroying my life. The insanity of that thinking! I didn't want anything to do with God. I had totally blocked Him out of my life. Yet, when my life collapsed around me, where did I point the finger of blame? Right at the One I had told to keep out of my life. How schizo is that?

Still, that's what I did. I straight-out told God that I hated

Him for all that He'd done to me. I cussed Him out and flipped my two middle fingers up to Him. I let Him know that He could just stay the hell away from me. I was just going to keep doing my own thing. I'm going to make money. I'm going to put whatever I want into my body. I'm going to use girls just to satisfy my own needs. I'm done looking for love. I'm done trying to find "the right one." Screw that—I've tried it. There's too much pain in relationships. Besides, you can't trust women anyway—they're all the same. As soon as you start loving one, she'll cheat on you or stab you in the back or kill your unborn kid. If God's got a problem with that, what do I care? He obviously doesn't care about me.

CHAPTER 2

Losing Control

It was soon after I'd had it out with God that I started my new job, and everything got really awesome really fast. My oldest brother, Raul, had founded Four Star Distribution, which was a group of four snowboard brands. Along with that project, he was working on starting a new skateboard company called C1RCA Footwear. Soon, all five brands dominated in their industries. The concept behind C1RCA Footwear was to build a brand around legendary pro skateboarder Chad Muska. That meant bringing together music, art, and the skateboarding culture to create a one-of-a-kind brand. There was nothing else comparable out there.

Since I was already producing music events, Raul, Chad, and I had a few conversations. The result was that I took a job as the head of music promotions and team manager for C1RCA Footwear. This was great timing for me. It got me to change my scenery. I was able to refocus and rebuild my life as I dedicated all my time to this new job. I put the nightmare that I'd just gone through behind me. I started working like a dog—long hours, seven days a week. But I loved it. I had finally found my dream job, and I was now doing what I was most passionate about. It was the perfect outlet for my creativity.

It was at this time that I birthed a new concept for a music festival with Muska called Skate Jam. It was the first of its kind, bringing skateboard culture, drum and bass and hip-hop music, and art together under one roof. With Wu Tang headlining, thousands of people poured in to watch the $10,000 best trick skate contest and listen to the bands. The C1RCA brand started invading the music scene.

It soon began showing up everywhere. Bands and celebrities were wearing our products. Media outlets, from MTV to all the music mags, were talking about us. We were being worn by Eminem, Deftones, Limp Bizkit, Ghostface Killah, Roni Size, and many others. This company was where I was putting much of my effort, and I was killing it. C1RCA was leading the way in the industry, and soon competing shoe brands were trying their best to match our success by copying our music initiatives. The plan was working and the long hours were paying off. I was psyched!

All the while, I was having the time of my life. I was twenty-two years old, and I was touring around the world, staying in the sickest hotels, going to the biggest music festivals and most exclusive parties, and working with the most popular bands on the planet. A couple of C1RCA team riders and I were invited by

Fred Durst, lead singer of Limp Bizkit, to the Playboy mansion, and we partied there for the band's record release party. Check that off the bucket list. We hung out at the mansion until pro skateboarder Adrian Lopez threw up by the peacocks, and then it was a wrap—we bounced. The Vivid porn girls hosted our snow brand parties, then came back with us to the house to continue the cocaine-fueled party. It was an insane life.

Toward the beginning of my C1RCA years, I wasn't using drugs at all and only drinking a little bit. I was really focused on my work. I wanted to kill it at my job, and I didn't want all the fog in my brain that came with the drugs. Besides, with how hard I was working, who had time to cut out and get wasted? That period of my life was as close to completely sober as I had been since I was a teenager.

I stayed straight for a few years. Then, like a cancer breaking through remission, the old ways began creeping back in. I'd be backstage at an event or at a club and someone would have cocaine. I'd justify to myself that a little bit wouldn't hurt. That "harmless" dabbling continued for a short while. A bump of cocaine here, a tab of ecstasy there. Once a month became twice a month, which became weekly until I got sucked back in again—it was like going over the falls on a surfboard. The apostle Peter wrote, "So be on guard; then you will not be carried away by the errors of these wicked people and lose your own secure footing" (2 Peter 3:17). If we're not watching for the temptations that are trying to destroy us, we'll step right into them and get taken out. It's like a fox walking into a trap. We let our guard down and suddenly the appetites of the flesh have us clamped in and we're powerless to break free.

As time went on, I found myself once again firmly in the

grip of my old ways. The final spiral began for me when there was a shift in the company. The brands were going through cuts and the entire music program got shut down. The music program was the whole reason I had been hired. My passion was in the music part of my job, but C1RCA decided to move away from that side of the business. My role shifted to just a team manager. Don't get me wrong—I loved my time hanging with those dudes, and I had some of the best times of my life traveling with them. We were and still are all brothers, and it was those amazing relationships that kept me there. But the challenge was gone; the creative drive was gone. I like to produce and create events—that's my passion; it's what I live for. Now my job had none of that.

With the excitement of my work fading, I began feeling like I was losing my purpose. I had more idle time on my hands and nothing good to do with those extra hours. I was looking for something to fill the void in my life. If you asked an outside observer, they'd say that I was living the dream. I had money, I had girls, I traveled. Wasn't that supposed to fill up the void and give me meaning? Instead, I found myself wanting something more—something real.

So much of what once had given me excitement just got really old and repetitive—going to the same countries over and over, putting on the same events, staying in the same hotels, hanging out in bars. Truth was I had gotten incredibly bored with life. Some might say, "Ryan, you had everything, man. How could that ever get old?" If you try to find your meaning in anything in this world—money, success, travel, relationships, sex, work—it's eventually going to fail you. We were created for something more, something greater, something bigger, something that makes a difference.

My life became a routine. I'd get up, go to work, go skate, get wasted, get up, go to work, go skate, get wasted. This was day after day after day. I got to the point where I didn't really care anymore if I lived or died. I wasn't suicidal; I just didn't care. Nothing satisfied me. Nothing made me happy. I felt like a dead man walking. I had no peace, no joy—nothing. Totally empty inside.

C1RCA sent me with their pro and amateur teams on a tour through Mexico, Costa Rica, and Panama City. The whole trip I was sneaking away and doing cocaine every night. The farther south you are, the purer the coke is. I was on a mission to try every bit I could get my hands on. Every day we'd do skate demos and autograph signings. Every night we'd go eat and finish at a bar. While everyone else was sticking to the alcohol, I was slipping away a couple of times every hour to the bathroom so I could dip my key into a bag of cocaine and snort it up my nose.

When we hit San Jose, Costa Rica, the drugs overpowered me and put me out of commission. After a night of alcohol and blow, I excused myself from the bar to go up to my room. I was so strung out I could barely think. I desperately needed some sleep. Every day I had been ending the night passed out on my bed, and passing out is not the same as sleeping. So, on my way to my room I did what any other drug-insane person would do when he needed to shut down—I dropped a bar of Xanax to counteract the cocaine. That way I wouldn't feel like I was coming apart at the seams the next morning.

I went to my room, did some more lines of cocaine, and passed out.

Later on, Adrian, Sierra, and a couple of other riders found me sprawled out on the bed—overdosed. There was cocaine all over my face and a bag on the table next to me. Adrian shook me and called my name, but I was totally unresponsive. Adrian got so freaked out that he called my parents back in California. Frantic, he told them what was going on and that he wasn't sure I was going to come out of this. Normally, this would be the time for someone to call the paramedics or the police. But remember, we were down in Central America and there were drugs all over the room. Chances are that if I came out of this, I and possibly a few of my other buddies would spend the next number of years in a Costa Rican prison. You going to make that call? Heck no!

Immediately, my parents began praying. There is power in prayer. It is our direct line to the Creator God of the universe. When people pray, God listens every single time. I'm not saying that He always does what we want Him to do. He's not a genie and prayer isn't a magic lamp. But we do know that every prayer we pray goes right to His ears, and He will always answer with what is best.

God heard my parents' prayers for my recovery. God answered, "Yes."

I woke up the next morning by God's grace. All the guys were like, "Dude, we thought you were dead last night." But I didn't really answer them. I was still high on the Xanax and wasted from the alcohol. I felt like I was floating. The team had gathered outside the hotel to go zip-lining out in the jungles where the movie *Predator* had been filmed. This was going to be one of the highlights of the trip for me, but when the van pulled up to the location, I spotted a hammock up on a hill hanging between two trees. It was just like you see in the movies—picture-perfect. The team went without me, while I slipped into the hammock. The cool breeze from the tropical forest felt amazing. I slept like I'd never slept before.

After one more night, I finally sobered up. That next day was a travel day, which landed us in Panama City. After the skate demo, I went to my hotel room at the Sheraton. I needed time by myself. Being alone can be sobering. It's when you're alone that you discover who you really are. It's just you and your mind. When you look in your own eyes in the bathroom mirror, all the masks are pulled away, and it's just you looking back at yourself. When I looked in that mirror, I didn't like what I saw. In my eyes I saw all the bad decisions I'd made, all the time I'd wasted being wasted, all the people I'd let down by losing control.

Then I did something that I hadn't done in years. I sat down on the edge of my bed and I prayed. Growing up in my dad's church, I'd heard a lot of versions of what is called "the sinner's prayer." This is the prayer that people say when they are tired of doing life their own way and decide to give their lives to Jesus. Pulling from those memories, I said, "Jesus, if You are real, I need You to prove it to me. I'll give my life to You. I need You to forgive me of my sins. I need You to come into my life and fill me with Your Holy Spirit. I can't do it my way anymore. I'm over it. I'll follow Your way if You show me You're real. Amen."

I sat there waiting for something to happen. I thought maybe Jesus would show up in my hotel room with rainbows, lightning bolts, and angels singing some chorus. He'd turn to me and say, "Ryan, I've been waiting for you, you dirty sinner." But that never happened. Jesus was a no-show. Just what I'd been afraid of. Just like I'd expected. "I knew You weren't real," I yelled, feeling the discouragement come back into my heart.

But even if I wasn't yet feeling like a great spiritual change had taken place, I knew that something had happened. The proof was that I was done with the drugs once and for all. I finally realized the toll they'd taken on my life, and I was tired of losing control. That night I found the team chilling in the Jacuzzi. The hardest thing for me to do was to confess and admit to them something that they already knew—I had an alcohol and drug problem. I told them I was committed to stopping it once and for all. When I heard the words coming out of my mouth, I was in shock. I had known that I had a problem, but I figured if I didn't admit it, then maybe it wasn't real. I was in denial. Once I said the words, there was no going back—the problem was real.

The weight of the world fell off my shoulders when I spoke those words to them. They supported me, and it was so awesome and encouraging to feel that from these friends who were like my family and who I highly respected. Something else came into my life in that moment—accountability. By telling them that I was done with all the substance abuse, I knew I couldn't jump back in again.

When I got back to my room, all the "what now?" questions started flooding my brain. What was going to happen when my brother Raul and his partner—the owners of C1RCA—found out? Was I still going to have my job? Did I still even want that job? Because by that point I was pretty much over it. And what did I need to do to get myself straight and stay that way? It was hard not to stress about the future.

The next day we flew back to the United States. Before leaving the hotel, I spent the morning up in my room thinking about God and the prayer I had prayed the day before. I knew that I had to be missing something. I'd seen my family and the peace and joy that they felt in their lives with God. Why wasn't I feeling those same things? There had to be an answer.

That's when a thought popped into my brain. I got out of bed and opened up the nightstand. In there I found a book with the words HOLY BIBLE written on it and PLACED BY THE GIDEONS stamped below. Lifting it out, I began to flip through the pages, thinking that if the prayer hadn't worked, then maybe this would help.

I was glad to discover that it actually was in English—well, almost in English. It was a King James Version, which to me was like reading Shakespeare. I've had ADD my whole life and was held back in school, so I have a very poor reading level. They even put me in special-ed classes because they didn't know how to deal with kids with ADD—or, as I call them, "Passionate and Driven Students Who Don't Fit the Box." So, as I read this Bible, it felt like most of the words were divided between those I didn't understand and those I couldn't pronounce. But still,

I knew that I needed to give it a shot. So, I stole the Bible and started reading it on the flight back to California.

Stealing that Bible from my Sheraton hotel room was the best decision of my life, because it changed me. I read that book for six hours straight on the flight back home. The skate team was probably tripping seeing me reading the Bible on the plane. They had known me for eleven years. They had to be thinking, "What is going on? Cocaine? Yes. Getting drunk out of his mind? Definitely. Chasing girls? Absolutely. But now the Cocaine Pirate is reading the Bible?"

Truth is, I couldn't put that book down. I figured that if God is real, then He had to be in that book, and I was going to find Him. By the time we landed—even with all the "thees" and "thous"—I felt like I had truly met God. And for the first time in seventeen years, I felt real peace. Little did I know then that what I was feeling was an encounter with God's presence—the Holy Spirit pouring into me.

So, just to make sure you haven't missed anything that's happened: I had totally screwed up my life by giving in to my body appetites, doing whatever felt good and totally living for myself. I came to the end of that nowhere way of living and I gave my life to Jesus. I repented, which means I turned away from living life my way and committed to start doing life God's way. I said, "Jesus, if You're real, then forgive me of my sins—all those things that I'm doing that are destroying me." He forgave me instantly, on the spot. I jacked the Bible from the hotel and in the pages discovered that Jesus Christ is real. He proceeded to fill me with the Holy Spirit, the Power from heaven, and the Holy Spirit gave me peace.

That Holy Spirit power is how God proves that He is real.

Jesus once said, "Anyone who is thirsty may come to me! Anyone who believes in me may come and drink! For the Scriptures declare, 'Rivers of living water will flow from his heart'" (John 7:37–38). You can't get that from any dead religion. It only comes through a relationship with the God and Creator of the universe.

That, my friend, is salvation right there. That's what it's all about. God is real and His name is Jesus Christ, and He wants a relationship with you. If you want to find out who He really is and not just what people say about Him, then find a Bible and read it (easiest way—find the Bible app and download it for free!). Do your own homework—don't depend on someone else's opinion. Find a Bible translation you like (I personally love the readability of the New Living Translation) and start reading the Gospel of John—the story of Jesus. You'll be amazed at what you discover. The Bible is the DNA of Jesus Christ and Jesus Christ is the DNA of holiness. It's in the Bible that we find all the answers to all the big questions of life: Origin—where did we come from? Purpose—why are we here? Morality—are there such things as right and wrong? Destiny—what happens to me when I die?

The Bible is truly the Word of God—100 percent accurate from Genesis to Revelation, from beginning to end. It's literally God's voice speaking to us. The apostle Paul wrote, "All Scripture is inspired by God and is useful to teach us what is true and to make us realize what is wrong in our lives. It corrects us when we are wrong and teaches us to do what is right. God uses it to prepare and equip his people to do every good work" (2 Timothy 3:16–17). That word "inspired" literally means "God-breathed." The Bible is straight from His mouth. You want to hear God speaking to you, telling you all the great things that He has waiting for you when you give yourself to Him? Crack open the Book.

———————

My first morning back home, I woke up with a song in my head. It's a simple song I had learned way back in Sunday school. Now here I am twenty years later singing these words to myself: "This is the day the Lord has made. I will rejoice and be glad in it." Those words were stuck in my brain, repeating over and over. I couldn't get them out.

I went outside to smoke a morning cig, and I started tripping out over these words. Why couldn't I shake this little kid's song? So I called my dad the pastor. I told him, "Dad, I gave my life to Jesus in Panama City. I'm done with living this wasted life. I've seized every opportunity and done everything I could have ever dreamed of. I've used every drug you can think of and I've been drinking like a fish. But now I'm done with all that and my allegiance belongs to Jesus the Messiah. The only problem is that now I've got this crazy song stuck in my head."

I've got to give my dad huge props. He could have absolutely freaked out over what I had just told him. He could have torn me up one side and down the other for all the terrible things I'd done in my life. He could have called me a worthless sinner and disowned me on the spot. But I knew he wouldn't. The reason I felt safe calling my dad is that he had never judged me. Even when I was at my worst, he always loved me and kept the door open to me. My mom was the same way. So when my dad answered with love instead of criticism, it was exactly what I expected and what I needed. He said, "Ryan, that's the Holy Spirit talking. He's calling you to Himself and He's got a great plan for your life." It's funny—that's what he had always said to me, even when I wasn't a Christian. He said it then, and he still says it now. "God's got a great plan for your life." He always believed it. This time I knew it was true. The same is true for you.

Just a quick aside—that little song is straight out of Psalm 118. Two thousand years later, people sang out another part of this same psalm as Jesus Christ rode a donkey into Jerusalem. The crowd was dancing and celebrating, singing, "Blessed is He who comes in the name of the Lord," because He had revealed to them that He was the true Messiah. Isn't it amazing that God gave me that same song right after He had shown me also that He was the true Messiah? It's more proof that God's voice is heard in the Word of God.

There's a verse in the Bible that says, "God showed his great love for us by sending Christ to die for us while we were still sinners" (Romans 5:8). Think about what that says. We were sinners. That means that we wanted nothing to do with God. He told us to live one way, and we decided our way was better.

Every time we do something that we know is wrong, it's like when I was giving God the finger. What would you do if somebody was flipping you off every day and doing everything exactly the opposite of what you wanted them to do? You'd be telling them not to do something, and then they'd immediately turn around and do it. You'd ask them to do something for you, and then they'd tell you what you could do with your request. That's us when we are living our own way and ignoring God.

But what Romans 5:8 tells us is that when we were cussing God out with the way we were living our lives, giving Him the finger and spitting in His face—that was the exact time when Jesus showed His love for us and died for us. And it's not because He's weak. It's not because He's so desperate for a relationship with us that He'll put up with any crap we give Him. He's not a codependent God. He got along just fine without us before, and He can keep on doing fine without us now.

No, the reason that Jesus Christ died for us even when we wanted nothing to do with Him was 100 percent out of love. The Bible says, "Love never gives up, never loses faith, is always hopeful, and endures through every circumstance" (1 Corinthians 13:7). God will never give up on you. It doesn't matter what you've done—God will never pull His love away from you. He will never lose faith in you. He'll always hold out the hope that with His help you'll be able to overcome whatever sin and circumstance is destroying your life. God sees the real you— the potential that He created in you. He sees you in the future fulfilling the mission that He's perfectly and specially created you for.

God will be there through all the great times and all the times you totally blow it. Think of the worst thing that you've ever done. Guess what—God is not shocked. He knows about it and He is still there loving you. There's no sin so big that it will chase God away. There's no drug you take or appetite you fulfill that's so far off the rails that He can't forgive you.

Forgiveness—that's what I found in that hotel room in Panama City. That's what you can find right where you're at now. It's the attraction of the Gospel message—the Good News. God is ready to forgive you, and He can't wait to reveal your purpose to you.

CHAPTER 3

Crossroads

A fresh start—it's like putting a big glass of muddy water under the kitchen faucet and turning the knob to high. The force of the clean liquid washes all the dirt and grime out until the water becomes clear and pure.

That's forgiveness. It's aiming that stream of God's grace onto your heart and letting all the bad choices and wrong things you've done rinse off until you're standing clean, pure, before the Lord. That's what happened to me when I asked Jesus for His forgiveness. The Bible says that when "we confess our sins to [God], he is faithful and just to forgive us our sins and to cleanse us from all wickedness" (1 John 1:9). I confessed; He forgave instantly—that's how God works. When He makes a promise, He keeps it every single time. So don't ever doubt.

As faithful as God is in keeping His promises to me, I've got to tell you I'm not even close to showing His standard of faithfulness back to Him. When I asked for forgiveness, I promised God that I would stop chasing my body appetites like I used to. I told Him I was going to clean up my life. I'm following you, God, 100 percent. And I kept that promise to Him—for a short time. But then those same old temptations and habits started coming back, and I began caving. Just because you become a Christian doesn't mean that you have arrived—that you have it all figured out and you'll be perfect for the rest of your life.

I was doing really well in fighting off the attacks. God instantly healed me of the desire for drugs and alcohol the first time that I prayed to Him. Even my language got better and I stopped dropping the f-bomb every third word. There was one area, though, that I kept taking direct hits on—it's what the Bible calls the lust of the eyes and the lust of the flesh.

For much of my life, I'd always dated a lot of girls. So hooking up was always right there for me. Even though I had a few girlfriends in the past, most of my relationships were just fun and games—nothing ever really deep. That kind of easy, carefree sex was simply a standard part of my old way of living.

When my life changed, I knew those habits had to change as well. The temptations were still there, but I was committed now to doing it the right way—to holding off on having sex until I was married to the woman of my dreams, the one that God created for me. Before, I'd always had it backward. I'd meet a girl, have a one-night stand, then decide whether or not I liked her. Now I had to shut that old way down.

A sexual habit is one of the hardest habits to break. With drugs or drinking, you'll pay for it the next day. There's a comedown or a hangover—you're totally miserable. With sex, the repercussions are long-term instead of immediate. There's nothing you feel physically that next day that tells you, "Dude, you really messed up last night." Instead, most of the consequences are emotional and spiritual, and they will often last a lifetime.

One day when those desires were at their greatest, I went back to pornography. I knew it was wrong, but I figured that watching porn was at least better than sleeping with girls. Besides, no one would ever know. This became my secret sin. But God sees everything.

All it took was that first time going back to the porn. I justified it by saying, "I'm not sleeping with anyone. Is it really so bad just to look?" The answer to that question is "Yes, it is really bad just to look." I'll talk about this in more detail in a later chapter, but suffice it to say that pornography is like throwing red meat to the beast of lust. With every piece it eats, it just wants more. Fighting against porn is one of the hardest battles you'll face, and if you're a man or woman struggling with it now, you know exactly what I mean.

My reason for bringing this up now is to show that just because you become a Christian doesn't mean that all your sin and bad habits instantly go away. Like I mentioned before, people think that God is like a genie. You rub His lamp, tell Him your wish to stop doing all the bad things, and He'll grant you a perfect life from that point on. But becoming a new person is a process. You're going to mess up along the way—guaranteed.

Forgiveness starts with conviction, and conviction leads to repentance. Conviction is a godly sorrow. Remorse is a worldly sorrow. It means you recognize that what you did was wrong. I can't tell you how many times when I was growing up I'd say, "I'm sorry," and the response would be, "You're only sorry you got caught." I hated hearing that, even though it was probably true. I wouldn't really feel like what I had done was all that wrong. I was more upset that I was getting in trouble for doing what I wanted to do and that I couldn't keep doing it some more.

There's an old saying about Christians that they like to sin on Saturday and pray on Sunday. Sadly, that's true for many. They go off drinking and using drugs and sleeping around, fig- uring that all they need to do is say the magic words, "I'm sorry, God," and He has to forgive them because the Bible says so. But that's not the way it works. The book of Galatians says, "Don't be misled—you cannot mock the justice of God. You will always harvest what you plant" (6:7). When we confess to God, He cares a lot more about our actions than about our words. It's a heart issue. He doesn't want to just hear "sorry"; He wants to see "sorry" in our hearts and in our minds. Lip service isn't enough. We need to work on making the changes that won't just set things right but that will make us the people God wants us to be.

In fact, that's what the word "confess" means. To confess means to say the same thing as God—to view things the same way He does. When we confess our sin, we are saying, "God, I agree with You that I shouldn't have done this. I feel terrible that I messed up this way and went against what You want me to do." That's what God is looking for—a heart that is truly sorry for what was done and that wants God's changes.

There's one more step in triggering forgiveness—repentance. Repentance says that we recognize that what we did was wrong, confess, and then commit to God that we are going to do our best to never do it again. It's like making a U-turn. You're flying down the street in one direction. You hit the brakes, spin the wheel, and start going back the other way. When we're following our appetites, we're racing away from God. With repentance, we U-turn away from the sin and head back, heart and mind, God's way. It's really that simple.

On the other hand, if we are asking forgiveness from God with the full intention of doing the exact same thing tomorrow night, then we're back to the Galatians verse about trying to mislead God. I've got news for you—you can't mislead God. He sees right through it. He knows empty words when He hears them.

What if you sincerely confess and repent, then end up failing and doing the same wrong thing the next night? That's a different story. We're all going to blow it. King Solomon—the wisest person ever—knew this to be true. He wrote, "Not a single person on earth is always good and never sins" (Ecclesiastes 7:20). So, if you're thinking that God is expecting absolute perfection from you and is going to kick you to the curb if you screw up, relax, don't trip—it's not true. As long as you keep coming back to Him, confessing your sins and truly committing to change, He will forgive you.

Remember the verse from 1 John? "If we confess our sins to [God], he is faithful and just to forgive us our sins and to cleanse us from all wickedness." Notice there's no limit listed for the number of times we will be forgiven. When we become believers in Jesus, we are not given a forgiveness punch card that reads, "When the numbers are gone, you're gone." That would totally suck! Instead, it's like an American Express black card—there are no limits. Whenever you turn back to God, He will be there waiting for you with open arms of forgiveness and acceptance.

———————

As free as God is with His forgiveness, oftentimes we are much less so. Sometimes that lack of forgiveness is toward ourselves and other times it is toward others. But it's forgiveness that lays the foundation for us to move forward in our lives, so we've got to find a way to accept it.

When I gave my life to Christ and was filled by the Holy Spirit, I knew that I was forgiven. The Holy Spirit made that clear to me by the peace He gave to me. I felt it flowing through me. The Bible says, "Therefore, since we have been made right in God's sight by faith, we have peace with God because of what Jesus Christ our Lord has done for us" (Romans 5:1). I knew that I had peace with God—that everything was now good between Him and me. The one I had trouble finding peace with was myself.

Let's face it—when you're in the midst of the party life, it can be epic! I had some insane times with my buddies when I was growing up and then later with the skate teams. The drinking, the drugs, the sleeping around—I did it all because I wanted to. And when I finished a day of partying, I couldn't wait to get up the next day and start it all again. That's the nature of sin—it's fun. If sin weren't fun, then nobody would be doing it.

The problem with the partying (and with any sin) is that all you're doing is thinking about that moment—what I want to do now, how I want to feel. You're not thinking of the consequences for tomorrow or next month or years down the line. You don't realize that what you are doing may come back to haunt you—and believe me, it will, and for me, it has.

Sometimes the long-term effects of sin can be physical. I know guys whose minds are messed up by the drugs they took. Drugs can affect the chemistry of your brain. I've got buddies who are dealing with bipolar disorder, schizophrenia, and all sorts of other psychological problems in part because of the drugs they took. I've got other friends whose bodies are all messed up because of the junk they dumped into them.

The effects of sin can also mess with you spiritually years later. I've been sitting there ready to give a talk to a bunch of students when a picture comes into my mind of some stupid, crazy thing I did years ago when I was wasted. It's usually followed by the thought, "Who are you to go talking to these kids? If they really knew some of the stuff you did, they'd probably throw you out of the school." That thought is not the voice of God. It's totally from Satan. He's the condemner. Guilt is one of the greatest tools he has for bringing us down.

The thing is we have no reason to feel guilty. That's right—we may feel bad about some of the things we've done, especially if our pursuit of our body appetites hurts other people. But feeling bad isn't necessarily a negative thing. Feeling bad can motivate us to do something to make the situation right. Feeling bad can keep us from ever wanting to do that dumb thing again.

Guilt is different. Guilt is paralyzing. Guilt says, "You are a bad person, and you'll always be a bad person." Those words are direct from the mouth of the enemy—Satan. He doesn't want you to forgive yourself. He knows that if we don't forgive ourselves, after a while we'll transfer that attitude to God. Soon we'll start feeling like there's no way He could forgive us, either. That will open a divide between God and ourselves because we'll start viewing God based on our own feelings rather than on what He says in the Bible.

God will always forgive. King David, a guy who slept with another man's wife and then had him killed to cover it up, knew about God's forgiveness. He wrote, "He does not punish us for all our sins; he does not deal harshly with us, as we deserve...He has removed our sins as far from us as the east is from the west" (Psalm 103:10, 12). How far is the east from the west? You can't measure it. Not only does God forgive our sins, but He forgets them. So, if He doesn't bring up your sins anymore, then why do you?

Chuck Smith, the founder of the Calvary Chapel movement, once said, "We can't know the peace of God until we experience the grace of God."[4] The word "grace" means receiving what we don't deserve. We don't deserve forgiveness from God, but in His grace He gave it to us because of what Jesus did on the cross. And He didn't just give it once. God's grace keeps giving and giving and giving.

That doesn't mean that we can just keep sinning with no consequences. Remember, God cannot be misled. Another way of translating Galatians 6:7 is, "God cannot be mocked. You reap what you sow." You can't just keep rubbing His grace in His face. There are consequences of sin. People get hurt, damage gets done, lives get trashed.

There's a positive side to that promise, too. If we sow good things, we will reap good things. If we forgive others, we'll be forgiven. If we love others, we'll be loved. It's our attitudes and actions that will usually determine how others deal with us, and that will always dictate how close we can be with God.

We will sin, even after we receive Jesus as our Savior and get God's forgiveness. But we don't make a habit of it. We strive to live for God. And when we do blow it, we know that we can run boldly to the throne of grace and find forgiveness there.

Jesus told a story about a guy who owed a king a boatload of money. It was so much that he would never be able to pay it off, no matter how hard he worked or how many side hustles he tried. The king said, "You can't pay me? Then it's slavery for you until you've paid your debt."

Immediately, the man dropped to his knees. "Please don't take me away! Have mercy on me! Have mercy on my family."

The king looked at the pitiful sight, and his heart was moved. "Okay, I'll forgive the money you owe me. You can go."

The dude freaked out. He gushed his thanks to the king, then left the palace dancing and celebrating. But in the middle of his celebration, an onlooker caught his eye. He thought, "Wait a minute—that guy owes me a hundred days' wages." Sprinting over, he caught the other man by the throat. As he shook him around, he demanded his money...now!

"But I don't have it," the second man pled as he gasped for air. "Please, just give me a little more time." But the first man didn't want to hear it and had him thrown into prison until he could pay his debt.

Word got back to the king, and he sent for the man whose debt he had forgiven. "You're a terrible person," the king said. "I forgave you all that money, and you wouldn't even forgive just a little debt? Seriously? Well, it's off to prison for you until you find a way to pay back every last penny you owe me."

Jesus finished this story by saying, "That's what my heavenly Father will do to you if you refuse to forgive your brothers and sisters from your heart" (Matthew 18:35).

For God, forgiveness is huge. It cost Him a ton to get the whole forgiveness thing moving. Jesus had to die on the cross for mercy to happen. But for Him, it was worth any price He had to pay for us to be able to be made right with Him. So, when we, in turn, aren't willing to sacrifice even a little by forgiving those who have wronged us, it's a big deal.

Right before Jesus told that story about the king and the guy who owed him money, His disciple Peter had asked Him a question. "Lord, how many times do we need to forgive someone who keeps on doing us wrong?" Then, feeling a little generous, he added, "I'd be willing to forgive him seven whole times. How about that?"

Jesus' reply showed how weak Peter's generosity was. "No, not seven times...but seventy times seven" (Matthew 18:22). For us non-STEM people, that's 490 times. Is Jesus saying that your 491st sin is unforgivable? No, He's saying that forgiveness never ends. His doesn't, and neither should ours.

When we don't forgive, there are consequences. First, Jesus says that we won't be forgiven ourselves. "If you forgive those who sin against you, your heavenly Father will forgive you. But if you refuse to forgive others, your Father will not forgive your sins" (Matthew 6:14–15). "But wait," someone might say, "didn't we read that if we confess our sins then God has to forgive us?" Exactly! But remember, repentance comes from a heart that says I want to stop doing things my way and start doing them God's way. If we aren't forgiving others, then that shows that we aren't ready to do things His way. That attitude comes from a relationship with God that's all talk and no heart. Therefore, it's not a real repentance. We've still got too much self-focus in our lives. We're like the guy who had his debt forgiven by the king but wouldn't forgive the one who owed him. When we remember how much God forgave us and what that forgiveness has given to us—peace with God and eternal life—it won't be such a huge deal to suck it up and forgive people who have done us wrong.

The other problem with not forgiving others is that it messes us up inside. When we hold on to the wrongs that others have done against us, it eats away at us and builds up bitterness, hatred, anger, and resentment. It can even cause physical harm and illness. There was a time a number of years ago after I had gotten my life straight that some ministry partners and friends hurt me badly. It was out of the blue and I hung on to that anger. Every time I saw them, I would feel the anger surface. Even when I wasn't with them, what they did would come into my mind and set me off. Soon, my anger started turning into bitterness, and I didn't like the thoughts that were coming to my mind. I knew something had to change. So, I prayed, "God, I really need help in forgiving them. I need a supernatural work in my life. Please step in and show me how to do what I need to do."

God is all about doing supernatural things in the natural realm. That's what He did when I prayed. He began to change my heart. It was not an overnight thing—it actually took years. Forgiveness can be like making a sword. You don't create a sword by putting a piece of metal in some fire, then pulling it back out and—bada bing, bada bang—there it is. The metal is heated, then laid on an anvil to get beaten. The hammer slams down time after time—moving the metal, shaping it and purifying it. Then the slowly developing weapon is slid back into the fire to have the whole process done again. It's only after many cycles of heating and hammering that a sword is created. As I prayed every day, revisiting the pain and anger, bitterness was hammered into forgiveness and forgiveness into love. With those who had hurt me, I am no longer a slave to anger and unforgiveness. My relationship with God even got stronger. That's the way forgiveness works—it ends up helping both the forgiven and the forgiver.

But what if someone does something to you that is unforgivable? I read recently that one in every three girls will be sexually abused before the age of seventeen, and one in every six boys. Every two minutes in the US a child is raped.[5] I know that for a lot of you reading what I've said about having to forgive everyone, your mind went right to the person who abused you. You're thinking that hell will freeze over before that scumbag receives your forgiveness. I totally get that. Let me introduce you to a friend of mine, Christina Boudreau, ambassador for The Whosoevers Movement (which I co-founded with Sonny Sandoval of P.O.D.) and the founder of Beauty Has No Size. Listen to her story, because she's been right where you're at.

CHRISTINA'S STORY

I was a church kid. I gave my life to Jesus when I was six years old. I lived with my parents and older sister. I didn't have any great problems to speak of. Then a family member began to rape me. For the longest time I refused to call what happened to me "rape." The word was too big, too violating. Being molested is terrible, but rape steals something from you. It wasn't until later in my life that the Lord showed me that I needed to call it what it was. A family member raped me over and over and over.

As I grew up, the abuse began showing itself in me. I hated women and began wearing baggy clothes because I connected more with the boys around me than the girls. All the girls were dressing up and putting pretty bows in their hair—that just wasn't who I was. I began wrestling with my sexual identity and began living a homosexual lifestyle. Meanwhile, I had major body image issues and developed anorexia and bulimia. I started cutting myself because I hated who I was. I remember standing in the shower feeling numb as I watched my blood run down the drain. When I was eighteen, suicide seemed to be the only answer left.

But that's when God got ahold of me again. He let me know that He loves me no matter what. He showed me that I am still beautiful to Him, no matter how broken I may be. He restored my value and my worth. I had a vision once of a butterfly in a painting. Its color had been all washed out. But then the Lord restored its color, then gave it a second coating—a double portion for all that I had been forced to endure. I was and always would be beautiful to Him. Think of that—let that truth sink into your brain: you are and always will be beautiful to God.

During my time of healing, God challenged me to forgive that family member. It was something that I knew I had to do. So, through much prayer I did it—or so I thought. But the wounds were just so deep. One night I was watching the movie *The Passion of the Christ*, which shows very graphically what Jesus had to endure on the cross. As I saw the pain and suffering He went through just so He could forgive me, I thought, "How can I not forgive that deeply, too?" I can love much, because I have been forgiven much. I can forgive, because He has forgiven me.

It has not been a smooth or easy journey. But God has given me the strength to forgive the way I need to. He even upped the challenge some more a little while back. "Lord, why?" I prayed. He replied, "Because I want you to see the face of the person who stole so much from you, and I want you to be able to see all the healing and restoration I've done in you." God can take the most difficult situation and use it for good.

I've completely forgiven that family member, but that doesn't mean that everything is perfect between us. They don't want anything to do with the Lord and are not interested at all in my forgiveness. It's God's job to make it right, not mine. I can only do my part. I leave the rest in His hands.

Unforgiveness to me is like pressing a bandage down onto a wound. It covers the damage but doesn't allow real healing. Forgiveness rips the bandage off and lets the blood flow. It's painful but purifying. It opens the door for cleansing, then scabbing, then healing. Sure, it may leave a scar, but as my Maker has shown me, it's my scars that make me beautiful.

Christina has taken what the devil tried to destroy her with and is now using it to speak to thousands of teens and adults each year as part of The Whosoevers Movement. Instead of breaking under her past, she is helping to change the life of others. That is the power of the Holy Spirit and of forgiveness. Christina says she is ready to reconcile with her family member if they are ever open to it. "Reconciliation" is just another word that means two people who are apart come back together. The Bible talks about it like this: "This includes you who were once far away from God. You were his enemies, separated from him by your evil thoughts and actions. Yet now he has reconciled you to himself through the death of Christ in his physical body. As a result, he has brought you into his own presence, and you are holy and blameless as you stand before him without a single fault" (Colossians 1:21–22). How rad is that! Amazing! When we are reconciled with God, everything is good between Him and us and we can enjoy once again being in His company.

It is our responsibility to work toward reconciliation. However, we are not responsible for the actions of others. Forgiveness is a heart thing while reconciliation is action. Forgiving is what brings you right with God, no matter what it does to your relationships with others. The Holy Spirit has led Christina to a place where she's ready to reconcile with her family member. But that started with her giving her pain over to Jesus, trusting in Him to heal her own heart and carry her through the hard process of forgiving.

God offers forgiveness to each of us. All we need to do to receive it is to ask with a sincere, repentant heart. No matter what you've done in the past, no matter what you're caught up in now, He is ready and excited to forgive you. All He asks in return is for you to forgive others like He has forgiven you.

CHAPTER 4

Punk Rock Jesus

Why me? Of all people in the world, why did God reach out to save me? If you think about it, it seems like there were so many others who deserved God's forgiveness so much more than I did. There were people who were living good lives—helping out the needy, going overseas with the Peace Corps, volunteering with the Salvation Army. Others were out doing all sorts of humanitarian work. Yet Jesus came to me—a party animal who loved to drink and do drugs and was always sleeping around. Back then, I could not have cared less if God had some plan for my life. But when I hit rock bottom, Jesus stepped in and lifted me back up and started making Himself known.

I was the exact kind of person that Jesus came to this earth to save. He didn't come for the clean and pure; He came for the gritty. If we look just at the church culture and all its history and traditions, it's easy to miss who Jesus really was. Listening to so many pastors and priests read the Bible in a lifeless monotone—with no passion, like they've never experienced the Savior they're reading about, like they're professors giving some boring lecture in a college economics class—how could anyone see the real Man behind the words of the New Testament? So many church preachers and teachers simply aren't presenting the real Jesus. The picture they give of Jesus is of some white-skinned, blue-eyed, silky-haired model sporting a clean white robe with a golden circle around His head and His feet never quite touching the ground. But that's the exact opposite of who He really was, although it's true that the Bible is not too clear about the silkiness of Jesus' hair. Jesus was a hardworking carpenter whose healing hands were probably covered with calluses from swinging a hammer. Based on the weather I experienced in Israel—heat, sunshine, wind, rain, blowing dust—all His traveling would have left Him with brown, leathered skin. Sleeping all those nights out in the wilderness likely would have matted up His typically curly Jewish hair, leaving it untamed, possibly with some sweet dreads in the back.

The religious establishment of Jesus' time had everyone intimidated. They could break a person without a second thought by throwing them out of the synagogue. But without blinking an eye, Jesus came in and confronted the establishment face-to-face. I like that about Him—He was no sissy or coward. He told it like it was. He said, "You guys are on a highway straight to hell, and your lies and arrogance are taking people with you."

The religious establishment said that you could only hang

out with good people. If someone is a dirty old sinner, then you avoid them at any cost. But Jesus said, "Forget that. I'm going to get my hands dirty—this is why I came. I'm going to the people who really need me. Since I've got a cure, I'm going to find me some people who are really sick, physically and spiritually." That's why He came to me in that hotel room in Panama City. And that's why Jesus is punk rock. Jesus' ministry was messy, and it still is today. The English evangelist Leonard Ravenhill is believed to have said, "Jesus did not come into the world to make bad men good. He came into the world to make dead men live!" Church traditions and rules and regulations mean nothing to Him. He just plain doesn't want you to go to hell! And He'll do whatever it takes to keep you from going there, including offering His own body up to the whips and the nails and the cross. It doesn't get more punk rock than that.

———————

If you're wondering why Jesus would ever want you, you're just the kind of person He's looking for. If you're wondering why Jesus wouldn't want you, then congratulations—you're probably a Pharisee. The Pharisees were the religious leaders of Jesus' day. They created a whole system based on staying as far away as possible from sin and sinners. Then Jesus came along and crashed the party. He started rubbing elbows and eating dinners with the very sinners that the Pharisees were telling everyone to stay away from.

Okay, side note: before we go further, let's quickly talk about sin. Sin at its most basic is doing anything that God doesn't want you to do. There are four words that the Bible uses for sin.

"Transgression" is defiance—a deliberate rebellion against God. "Sin" means to miss the mark or not meet God's requirements. "Iniquity" comes from the word for "crooked" and implies perverseness. "Deceit" is anything against the truth.[6] This deceit is why Jesus calls Satan "the father of lies" (John 8:44). In another place, Jesus says, "'You must love the LORD your God with all your heart, all your soul, and all your mind.' This is the first and greatest commandment. A second is equally important: 'Love your neighbor as yourself'" (Matthew 22:37–39). So, sin is anything that is not loving toward God and toward others. There are places in the New Testament where sin is defined in more detail (Galatians 5:19–21; 2 Timothy 3:2–5), but we pretty much know deep down what is right and wrong.

What you need to know about sin is that everybody you see walking into a church building on a Sunday morning is a sinner. Everybody sins. And if you sin, then you are by definition a sinner. So, if you're thinking that you would be the only sinner sitting in a church service, you are mistaken. I'm not saying that sin is no big deal. God hates sin, but He 100 percent loves sinners. The difference with many of the church people you see is that they've had their sins forgiven because of Jesus dying on the cross. Jesus paid the penalty for your sin so that your sin isn't held against you anymore. What Jesus asks in return is that you change the way you live, do your best to stop your sinful lifestyle, and start living for Him. Whenever you read me going on about sin, this is what I'm talking about.

Now, back to punk rock Jesus. If you've ever spent time in church, you may have heard one of Jesus' most famous sayings: "Be in the world but not of the world." Problem is Jesus never actually said it. In fact, no one in the Bible said it. However, we do see Jesus living it, which means it's a good philosophy for our lives. Most of Jesus' ministry was around the Sea of Galilee, which is also called Galilee of the Gentiles. In the Jewish eyes of that day, anyone who wasn't a Jew was a dirty, bacon-eating Gentile—the sinners of all sinners. The Pharisees were saying, "Keep away from the sinners, and if you don't, we'll figure that you're a sinner, too"—total guilt by association. Jesus, however, was saying, "Healthy people don't need a doctor—sick people do. I have come to call not those who think they are righteous, but those who know they are sinners" (Mark 2:17). The problem with a lot of people in churches today is that they are speaking like Jesus, but they are living like Pharisees—they are talking the talk but not walking the walk.

I once saw a story about this TV preacher who owned three private jets. When a reporter asked him how he could justify spending money on these planes instead of flying commercial like everyone else, he basically said that he couldn't be expected to spend hours in a long tube filled with a bunch of demons and then step out and preach the Word of God. The dude didn't want to get that sinner taint. But those commercial planes are filled with the same sinners that he should be preaching to. Think of the logic—I'm going to avoid telling a bunch of sinners the truth about something they don't know, just so I can be holy enough to tell a bunch of church people stuff they already know. What a shame!

That's why in the Bible you always see Jesus hanging out with the sinners. When I started digging around trying to figure out who these sinners were, I realized that they were me. They were the wolves of Wall Street. They were living the pirate life, always trying to please the body appetites. These were the ones that Jesus was looking out for. These were the people that He was on a mission for. He was all about reaching the lost at any cost—even if it made Him guilty by association.

In Mark 1, Jesus was starting His ministry, or His mission on earth. That's what ministry is—it's following the plan that God has put forward for you to serve Him and help people. The Father had directed Jesus to do certain things while He was here on earth. He also has things that He wants you to accomplish during your life. This is your ministry, or mission.

So, John the Baptist was baptizing people, and Jesus went to him and got dunked in the river. As soon as He came up, He saw the heavens open and the Holy Spirit flying down to Him looking like a dove. Then God the Father said, "You are my dearly loved Son, and you bring me great joy" (Mark 1:11). The Father, Son, and Holy Spirit were all together there at the river.

From then on, Jesus, the doctor with a cure for sin, was on a rescue mission for sinners. But before He started His public ministry, the Holy Spirit drove Jesus out into the wilderness. That driving or compelling force is something that the Spirit can provide for each of us. If we want Him to use our lives, He'll lead us right to our calling. Jesus went out there to pray hard and fast ferociously for forty days. Now, that is hard-core! He knew that before He could do God's will, He had to be prayed up and fasted up and in tune with the Holy Spirit.

If we're going to reach the lost at any cost, we've got to do the same. If you're a Christian and you're wondering why you're not leading your friends or any strangers to Christ, take a look at your prayer life and at how much time you're spending in the Bible. How much do you know about Jesus and His character? Is your connection with God based on traditions and rules—are you just going through the motions and rituals? Or is it grounded in a relationship? A relationship with God should be like it is with your best friend—always talking to them and listening to what they have to say. They can hear your heart and you can hear theirs. When you get going strong with God, the Spirit will give you all you need to make a difference.

Satan knew that after fasting and praying, Jesus was ready for war, so now was his time to show up. He started tempting Jesus with the lust of the eyes, the lust of the flesh, and the sinful pride of life. These are the same things that he tempts us with. Satan understood that once Jesus started His ministry, it would be the beginning of a huge defeat for him. So Satan tried to disqualify Jesus at the starting line. But Jesus battled Satan with the Word of God. When you decide that you're going to start following and serving God, Satan is going to show up against you, too. He'll want to knock you down, make you fail, make you feel worthless. But you've got the Word of God on your side. This makes all the difference.

Remember this: when Satan attacks, he likes to play mind games. But we have the Holy Spirit, and He will bring the Word of God to mind so you can battle back the way Jesus did. You can take the lies that you hear from Satan and put them next to the Bible verse that Jesus is dropping into your mind through the work of His Spirit. By doing this, you put Satan and the Word of God in the octagon, and Satan is going to tap out. He has to. Fact! Satan is one of God's creations, and Jesus is the

Creator (John 1:1–4). Satan has to bow because he's no match—not even close.

After putting Satan in his place, Jesus came out of the wilderness and started recruiting disciples. Then one Sabbath, He went to a synagogue. The synagogues were like the Jewish churches of the day. Jesus went in and started teaching, and the people were tripping. "The people were amazed at his teaching, for he taught with real authority—quite unlike the teachers of religious law" (Mark 1:22). The religious system of the time was broken and the teaching was dead. God had put the Pharisees and leaders in place for a reason. They were to be like farmers. They'd till the soil of Israel so that it would produce spiritual fruit—a crop of godly Jews who loved and served God. So, the religious leaders were supposed to care for the people and water them and nurture them. But instead of serving the people, they got corrupt. They thought they were better than the rest of the Jews. Then they started ripping everyone off.

At one point, Jesus called them out for it. He said they were like whitewashed tombs—looking all clean-cut and proper on the outside but totally dead inside. He told them, "What sorrow awaits you teachers of religious law and you Pharisees. Hypocrites! For you shut the door of the Kingdom of Heaven in people's faces. You won't go in yourselves, and you don't let others enter either. What sorrow awaits you teachers of religious law and you Pharisees. Hypocrites! For you cross land and sea to make one convert, and then you turn that person into twice the child of hell you yourselves are!" (Matthew 23:13–15). Talk about punk rock! Can you imagine how the people were freaking out? Nobody said that to a Pharisee. Everyone was way too scared of them. But not Jesus—He was not timid or weak. He was power under control. A Man who knew His strength and used it when it was necessary.

The Pharisees didn't know how to teach the truth. For them, teaching meant reading a little bit of the Bible and then talking about what a bunch of old rabbis and teachers said about it. Punk rock Jesus comes in and says, "Forget about some dude's opinion about this. Let's look at what it really means." The people loved it. This is the "teaching with real authority" that they were talking about back in our Mark 1 passage. They couldn't get enough and they started gathering around Him from all over just to listen.

While Jesus was teaching at that synagogue, a demon-possessed man started yelling at Him. Jesus told the demon, "Be quiet! Come out of the man" (Mark 1:25). The man screamed, dropped to the ground, and the demon took off. The people couldn't believe what they had just seen! As soon as they left the synagogue, they began telling everyone they knew about this Jesus guy. Meanwhile, Jesus went to the home of Peter and Andrew, two of His disciples, and healed Peter's mother-in-law. Then massive crowds showed up at the house and He spent hours healing people and casting out demons. That's the difference between dead religion and the power that comes from a relationship with God. Are you going through the motions or are you letting your God do great things through you?

––––––––––

It had been a full day for Jesus—teaching the people, pissing off some Pharisees, casting out a demon, healing a mother-in-law, then healing a bunch of others and casting out many more unclean spirits. Jesus crashed for the night but got up early the next morning. He needed to talk to the Father God so He could find out what to do next. Word was out about Him, and His fame was growing. He had no doubt that He was going to get slammed with people in need. So He went out to get Himself dialed in with the Father.

If we're going to make a difference in this world—do stuff that really matters—we need to prepare ourselves, too. When you're reading and praying and fasting, signs and wonders are going to follow. Even if you're not looking for them, the Holy Spirit will still show up and blow your mind.

A few years back, I was speaking at a weekly study I led at Calvary Chapel Costa Mesa. I was standing there and this girl came up with a dog. I was like, "What's up with the dog?"

She said, "I have seizures. They took my license away and I have to have the dog."

"Seriously? Let's pray for God to heal you."

We prayed; then she went on her way. Years later, this girl DMs me on Instagram. She says, "Remember me? You prayed for me at your weekly study. Since that day I have not had one seizure and now I have my license back."

Amen! Isn't God awesome! I wasn't thinking, "Yeah, man, I totally have the gift of healing. Come check me out." What happened to that girl had nothing to do with me. All I did was say let's pray and see what God does. It was all God. Jesus wants to show Himself to people. He was saying, "I love this girl and I want to touch her life." Again, that's punk rock Jesus, always going against the odds and shaking things up. The doctors said you're going to have seizures the rest of your life. The government said you can't drive anymore. Jesus said, "We'll see about

that." Then He stepped in and did what He had decided to
do—never mind that it was totally impossible. And when we
get ourselves ready by reading the Bible and praying and fasting,
we'll be the ones that God uses through the work of His Holy
Spirit to do His amazing miracles.

After that day at the synagogue and possibly Peter's house,
Jesus began teaching and healing around the Sea of Galilee,
which isn't so much a sea as it is a really big lake up in the north-
ern part of Israel. As I mentioned earlier, another name people
used for the sea was Galilee of the Gentiles, because there were
so many non-Jews living up there. There was also a lot of pagan
worship and occult practices. At that time, Jews and Gentiles
didn't like each other. In fact, they hated each other. Jews stayed
away from Gentiles and Gentiles stayed away from Jews. They
were like rival gangs, and when they clashed, it wasn't pretty.
So, where did Jesus spend most of His three years of ministry?
The Sea of Gentiles, right where the establishment said not to
go. Again, Jesus is breaking man-made rules and old traditions.

One day as He was heading back to His home base in the
town of Capernaum, He came across a leper who needed healing. A leper—a man with leprosy—came and knelt down
in front of Jesus. Leprosy was a nasty and lonely disease that
was highly contagious. Anyone who had it was forced to stay
away from people and yell, "Unclean," whenever anybody got
too close.

Jesus looked at him and was "moved with compassion"
(Mark 1:41). Even though He had never met him, Jesus loved
this guy and was heartbroken at the terrible life he'd had to live.
So, Jesus reached out and touched the man. You're probably
saying, "Ryan, are you kidding me? He touched the diseased,

contagious dude?" Yes, He did! Jesus touched the man. Nobody touched a leper. You want one sure way to get leprosy yourself? Go give a leper a big bear hug. It had probably been years since this man had felt the touch of another human being. But Jesus knew what he needed—some healing, but also some love.

So, Jesus put his hand on the man and the guy got healed on the spot. An incurable disease was cured. That's exactly what Jesus does with us. We have an incurable disease called sin— all that stuff that we've done wrong throughout our lives. If we can't get rid of all the anger, bitterness, drugs, alcohol, greed, and porn addiction—all the things we war with—we're eventually going to die of it. But then Jesus steps in and gives you that love touch and suddenly it's all gone. He takes away all the junk that is bringing you death and He replaces it with life. In other words, He will destroy everything that is destroying you. And all we need to do to get that healing is the same thing the leper did—just drop on your knees in front of Jesus and ask.

Still not convinced that Jesus was full-on antiestablishment? Let me give you two more stories that'll show that if Jesus were doing ministry today, He'd probably look like you and me.

At the beginning of Mark 2, Jesus was back at Peter's house in Capernaum. Word got around fast and soon the place was packed. People were everywhere—inside and out. There were four types of people there. First, there were the seekers. They were there looking for truth. Today, you've got the same kind of people all around. They're checking out New Age, Wicca, Satanism, Buddhism, Hinduism, Islam, Mormonism—anywhere they can go to find answers to their spiritual questions. These seekers who were surrounding Jesus had come to the right place. In John 14:6, Jesus said, "I am the way, the truth, and the life. No one can come to the Father except through me." You're looking for truth? You found Him.

A second group was the spectators. They were looking for a show. They wanted to see people getting healed—maybe even watch as a demon came flying out of somebody. If the show was good enough, then maybe they'd sit through the sermon.

A third group was the spies. These were the religious leaders of the time. They were totally critical of anything that wasn't exactly according to their very strict ways. They had come looking for a reason to take Jesus down.

Once you start becoming critical, it's hard to back out of it. It eats away at your soul and becomes part of you. There are a lot of critical Christians around whose one joy in life is talking against and tearing down other Christians who don't look like them or worship like them or believe exactly what they do. Some of these critics love to attack through the computer. My friend Brian "Head" Welch calls them keyboard gangsters.

Amazingly, there are people who actually believe what some random "Christian" critic writes on the internet, even though they know nothing about that person. My question is who the heck is this dude and what have they done for the kingdom of God? The likely answer: zero, at least compared to the people that they attack and judge and talk trash about. What's worse are the readers of these internet posts who believe it all without having any background on the writer or even knowing whether the person is credible. All you know is a screen name—and that's probably not even their real name.

There are some church people that got their Bible school and seminary on. They put the time in, and they got their paper up on the wall. There's nothing wrong with getting a biblical education—in fact, it can be a great thing. But so many come out of their schools thinking that they know it all. The Bible says that knowledge puffs up (1 Corinthians 8:1). This means that you've got all these swollen-headed Christians thinking that heaven is only going to be filled with people who look exactly like them. Imagine their faces when they get to their heavenly mansion and see me with my moving truck unloading next door.

"Wait, you guys made it?"

"Yeah, dude, we made it. And guess what. There are some Pentecostals across the street and some Lutherans next to them. I even saw some Jesus-loving, Spirit-filled Catholics a block over. And we're all here with you for eternity. Oh, and by the way, barbecue at Brian Welch's house today..."

The last group at the house was the sick, and that's where our story kicks in. Four guys arrived carrying their paralyzed buddy on a mat. They had heard about Jesus and His healing power, so they had packed their friend up and trekked across town. But now they saw the crowds surrounding the already filled house. There was no way they were going to be able to push and elbow their way through the front door. In fact, there was no way they were even going to make it to the front door.

But there was also no way they were going to give up. Their friend was in desperate need. He couldn't eat by himself or drink by himself. He couldn't even get dressed or go to the bathroom by himself. In that culture at that time, this guy was as good as dead. The one hope he had was to get to Jesus. There had to be a way in—the friends just had to figure it out.

You ever been in a situation where you want to get into a concert, but it's sold out—or, like me, you had no money? What do you do? You sneak in! You jump the fence like my friends and I did at Lollapalooza. We were high on LSD and all we could think was that we had to see Alice in Chains and Primus. So, we hopped the fence, sprinted past the security guards, and we were in. This dude's friends knew they had to get their boy in, so they scouted the area and strategized until one of them said, "How about we break in through the roof?" The others looked at him with grins on their faces. "Heck yeah! It's going down right through the roof!" High fives all around.

"All right, all we really need is some rope. You got any rope?"

"Yeah, right here in my pocket where I always keep it. Of course I don't have any rope!"

So they went to the neighbor's house and knocked. "Hey, man, you got any rope, and maybe a ladder?"

The neighbor answered, "What do you need it for?"

"We're going to lower our boy through the roof of the house next door."

"You're crazy; I'm not giving you rope," the neighbor said. "That's Peter's house. If he finds out I helped you bust through his roof, he'll come over and knock me out. You ever seen him? Peter's a gnarly man. And that motley crew of disciples he hangs out with—I don't know what's up with those guys." The neighbor tried to shut the door, but one of the friends slipped his sandal in.

"Come on, just give us the rope and a ladder. We won't say where we got it."

The neighbor thought for a moment, then said, "Fine. Here, take it. I'm going to hide out here with my blinds down. If Peter finds out, I'm coming for you and your friends before he gets to me."

The friends carried the ladder, the rope, and their buddy to the back of the house. A couple of them climbed to the roof. They tied their friend onto the mat, then started hauling him up. Have you ever lifted deadweight? It's not easy. They were probably huffing and puffing, while below you've got people gathering around, helping to push the man up. Finally, they got him onto the roof. The houses of that time were made of adobe, like what you find in New Mexico. So the friends started digging.

Inside, Jesus was teaching. As He was talking, the people heard this ruckus on the roof. Everyone looked up, except Jesus—He already knew what was going on. Then dust started falling, then some little adobe chunks. Jesus brushed off the top of His head, looked up with a big smile, and probably just laughed, stoked at these guys' faith. Soon a hole opened, and a face peeked through looking like an angel with the swirling dust and the sun in the background. As the powder settled, they could see that the angel was actually dirty and very sweaty. Everyone was whispering back and forth, trying to figure out what was going on. Well, everyone except Peter, who was thinking, "These dudes are done! Where's my bat for home intruders? These fools are about to get smoked!"

They finally got the hole big enough—imagine how big it needed to be to let a man-sized mat through. Let's face it: the whole roof was destroyed. The friends started lowering their friend down. He was lying flat, so he couldn't see a thing until he got to eye level. He spotted Jesus and thought, "Oh yeah!" Then he saw Peter behind Jesus and thought, "Oh man."

The room was dead silent as people waited to see what Jesus

would do. "Seeing their faith, Jesus said to the paralyzed man, 'My child, your sins are forgiven'" (Mark 2:5). Two things: First, neither the paralyzed man nor his friends had said a word. Jesus just looked at them and saw their faith. Jesus knows our hearts. He knows when we're following Him. He knows when we're playing a game.

Second, Jesus said, "Your sins are forgiven." Not "Your body is healed" or "Paralysis, be gone." The paralyzed dude's friends were probably like, "Whoa, whoa, whoa—his sins are forgiven? That's it? Listen, we are not carrying this guy all the way back home! We need our boy to walk!" But Jesus knew that this guy was in a terrible place in his life because of the sin that had gotten him there. A lot of Bible teachers think that the man likely had syphilis, which is an STD. It attacks the brain, then slowly goes after the nervous system until it paralyzes its victim. Or maybe he was just out one night and got wasted drunk and did something stupid and ended up breaking his neck. You hear about those kinds of stories all the time. But whatever sin it was that got him into this position, this man had to wake up every day thinking, "Why, why, why did I ever do that?" So, for him to hear "Your sins are forgiven" had to be the best news ever.

Jesus had addressed the main problem. You could say to me, "Ryan, pray for me that I stop using drugs." I can pray for you and God can take away the drugs, but now you're just a sober sinner. Your body may be better, but your soul is still dead and you haven't turned off the highway to hell—and that's no good. The most important thing in our lives is being forgiven and having a relationship with Christ. That's what allows us to get to heaven. Imagine if the guy got up from his mat and thought,

"Okay, I got away with that. Next time I'm going to be a little more careful." Dude, I can totally relate to that.

But while the paralyzed guy was lying there celebrating and his friends were looking down and freaking out, the Pharisees were standing to the side and they were steaming. They were thinking, "What is he saying? This is blasphemy! Only God can forgive sins!" (Mark 2:7). What they said was very wrong, but it was also exactly right. Saying it's blasphemy is wrong, because Jesus is God. Saying only God can forgive sins is right, because Jesus is God. The religious establishment was saying, "You can't do this." Jesus said, "Stand back and watch Me."

The Gospel of Mark says that Jesus knew their angry thoughts, so before they even had a chance to say anything, He answered them. "'Why do you question this in your hearts? Is it easier to say to the paralyzed man "Your sins are forgiven," or "Stand up, pick up your mat, and walk"? So I will prove to you that the Son of Man has the authority on earth to forgive sins.' Then Jesus turned to the paralyzed man and said, 'Stand up, pick up your mat, and go home!'" (Mark 2:8–11).

I could say to you, "My friend, your sins are forgiven." You might believe me, but you could never be sure. Your sins are inside of you—how would you know whether or not I actually got rid of them? But by Jesus telling the paralyzed man to take up his mat and walk, He's demonstrating that He is God and that He has full power to forgive sins. It's not blasphemy—He's totally the right guy for the right job.

The man stood and picked up his mat and everyone started freaking out—everyone except the religious people. They totally ignored it. They saw the work of God right in their faces, but they refused to accept it, which is evident as time goes on. Again, this reminds me of all the internet Pharisees who are always trolling me and The Whosoevers and other ministries that are in the trenches on the front line. People are getting saved. People are getting healed. Jesus is moving in miraculous ways, but they choose to doubt the evidence of God. Just because we look different from them, just because we do ministry different from them, just because some of our backgrounds are a bit sketchy, they say, "Heathen! Sinner! Blasphemer!"

To which I say, "Dude, take it up with God. He's the One saving all these people. He's the One healing them. I'm just along for the ride." Or, since they're acting like Pharisees, I'll give them the words of a Pharisee. When all the other religious leaders were attacking the disciples, this one old guy, Gamaliel, said, "So my advice is, leave these men alone. Let them go. If they are planning and doing these things merely on their own, it will soon be overthrown. But if it is from God, you will not be able to overthrow them. You may even find yourselves fighting against God!" (Acts 5:38–39).

So, Jesus healed the man right in the middle of the room. I love this picture. The place was so jam-packed that the guy was having to weave his way out of the room—wedging between people, accidentally smacking folks in the head with the mat poles. Meanwhile, Jesus was just looking at the Pharisees, like, "What? I told you, now check it out. Dude's walking. I told you, my name is Jesus Christ, and I'm the faith healer." Up top, the man's friends were watching the whole thing and probably saying, "Thank God—literally! Glad we don't gotta haul him back up. Hey, Peter, my man can work now—he'll be here first thing in the morning to fix your roof."

The religious establishment said, "You have to act like us to be right with God." Punk rock Jesus said, "No, man, you just got to believe." The religious establishment said, "Only God can forgive sins." Punk rock Jesus said, "You got that right, and it's nice to meet you."

———————

Next time we see Jesus, He was cruising by the lake. Crowds were following Him, and He was teaching as He went. As He was walking, He spotted a guy working in a booth alongside the road. Have you ever seen people whose eyes are so vacant you know they're empty inside? That's what Jesus saw in this man—an absolute vacancy in his heart. Not that you'd know it from the outside. On the surface, he looked like a total baller.

The guy's name was Levi and he was a tax man, which meant he was a Jew who worked for the Roman government. The Romans would say, "Hey, you've got to bring in ten thousand dollars per month for us. Anything you can get after that is yours." If you're offered that deal, what are you going to do? You're going to rip people off every day from Sunday. That was Levi—stealing from the people, living the life, getting drunk, partying, doing what sinners do. He'd have moms coming with their kids, old folks hobbling in barely having any food to eat, and he'd skim everything he could from them to pay his own bills.

Jesus knew who Levi was—a sinner and a slimeball—but still He walked up to him and said, "Yo, Tax Man, follow Me." Now Levi had a choice. On one side he had a nice government job paying big cash—on the other was major uncertainty, wandering around with a traveling preacher and a bunch of guys who smelled like fish. But then taking a closer look, there was something they had that he was lacking—passion and purpose. Dude didn't think twice. He counted the cost and He left everything behind for Christ.

To celebrate this huge change in his life, Levi threw a party. Who did he invite? The holier-than-thou religious people? Heck no. Levi invited his bros. "Later, Levi invited Jesus and his disciples to his home as dinner guests, along with many tax collectors and other disreputable sinners. (There were many people of this kind among Jesus' followers.)" (Mark 2:15). I love that last sentence! These were His people. Looking around Levi's crib, did Jesus say, "Uh, Levi, think you could find a better group of friends?" Of course not, because Jesus' own crew was a bunch of knuckleheads. His disciples were a bunch of blue-collar, filthy fishermen who certainly didn't fit in with the beautiful crowd. He even had this guy with him named Simon who was a Zealot. The Zealots were this radical group who were all about overthrowing the government. Simon was like that one buddy who every time he smokes weed he starts talking conspiracy theories and about sticking it to the man.

There was one other dude who became part of the crew named Matthew. His past was definitely jacked. Seems he used to be a tax collector and went by a different name—Levi. That's right, Levi the tax collector was the same Matthew who became one of Jesus' disciples and ended up writing the first book of the New Testament. See what God can do with us messed-up sinners and with ordinary men and women?

The religious leaders, though, were looking at this bad-to-the-bone cast of characters and they were disgusted. They asked,

"Why does he eat with such scum?" (Mark 2:16). Again, they were totally missing the point. They wanted to stay in their safe little bubble. They didn't want any of that sinner's taint to rub off on them, like when you're a kid and you didn't want to touch any of the girls in case you'd end up getting their cooties. But once again, Jesus went against the establishment—He really was sticking it to the man. He was hanging with the ones who needed Him, not with the ones who thought they didn't. He said to the Pharisees, "Healthy people don't need a doctor— sick people do. I have come to call not those who think they are righteous, but those who know they are sinners" (Mark 2:17). We're called to take the healing power of Jesus Christ to those who are soul-sick. But it's never going to happen if we keep our- selves safely locked up in our airtight, vacuum-sealed, germ-free churches. Guess what—following Jesus is messy and it's fun!

Don't get me wrong—I'm not saying that all churches are bad. There are a huge number of great churches with hearts for the lost, whose doors are open to anybody who walks in. But there are also others who have lost their purpose and are busy building walls to keep the holiness in and the riffraff out. These are the ones who always have their knives out, ready to take down Christians who wander out into the sinful world.

Brian "Head" Welch, one of the founding members of Korn, faced this church Pharisee backlash when he decided to rejoin his band. After Head gave his life to Christ, he left Korn for a while. He had to get himself solid and figure out what Jesus wanted from him. When God made it clear to him that he was supposed to go back to the band, he did. The Pharisee commu- nity exploded. If you read some of the articles and social media posts about him, you would have thought he'd driven a monster truck through a puppy farm. "How could a Christian go back to a sinful environment like that?" they cried. Maybe it's because a sinful environment is where the sinners are. Maybe it's because it's the sick who need the cure. After every Korn concert, Head is sharing Christ and he's leading people to the Lord.

If you've got the soul sickness, if you're empty and are looking for someone to fill that void, Jesus is there for you. He's got His eye on you. His love for you goes way beyond any wrong thing you've ever done and will do in the future. All you have to do is look at Jesus' life and you'll see that you are the exact kind of person that He wants a relationship with. If you ask for His forgiveness, He'll give it to you. If you give Him your life, He'll take it and make something amazing out of it.

If you've already been cured of the sin disease and you've been made right with Christ, then it's time to start being part of God's plan to heal others. To do that, you've got to be with the sick. It's when you go to the darkest places that the light shines the brightest. Some say, "Oh, I can't hang out with them. They're always dropping f-bombs. They're always saying these bad things." Of course they are. What world do you live in? That's everywhere. Are you scared to hang out with your friends because of the way they talk? Are you going to be fine if, when you get to heaven, you have to say, "Well, sadly all my friends are in hell now because I couldn't hang out with them since they were always dropping the f-bomb and stuff"? Who cares what they say? I'm always around people who talk like that. I'm not offended or defiled by their words. I've got the Holy Spirit in me. Jesus is my King and He reigns in my life. Bad words aren't going to break through that protection. I'm just there loving them and letting them see that Christ loves them, too.

One of Jesus' brothers, Jude, wrote, "And you must show mercy to those whose faith is wavering. Rescue others by snatching them from the flames of judgment. Show mercy to still others, but do so with great caution, hating the sins that contaminate their lives" (Jude 22–23). If you're going to rescue people from hell, you've got to be at the gates of hell. If you're pulling them from the flames, you're probably going to end up smelling like smoke. But Jude also says to "do so with great caution." That's the warning, and we've got to pay attention to it. If you're getting over alcoholism, don't go right back into a bar. If you're getting over pornography, don't start up a strip club ministry. Be smart. Grow in your faith. Get strong. When you're ready, the Holy Spirit will lead you where He wants you to go.

Why did Jesus save me? Because He loves me. While you may feel like the religious establishment has turned its back on you, Jesus is not the establishment. He will never turn His back. In fact, He's facing you right now, arms open, saying, "Let Me give you hope. Let Me give you peace. Come home."

CHAPTER 5

Identity Crisis

Imagine one day you get the news that your family is moving, and it's not just to another city but to another country. You're going to have to leave your school in the middle of the year and try to hit the ground running in a brand-new one. You won't know any of the other students—you won't even know the language they're speaking. Imagine how lost and out of place you'd feel.

That's what it felt like when I walked into a church after becoming a Christian. Here I was in a new place filled with all these people who looked a lot different than me. They were speaking a strange language—Christianese—saying things like "blessing my socks off" and words like "hallelujah" and "anointed," and talking about "hedges of protection" and "words of prayer." Even though my parents were Christian, I never really paid attention to this Christianese language. Now here I was wondering what everyone was saying.

When the pastor started preaching, he'd tell the people to turn to some passage in the Bible. All the people around me would turn right to it, and I'd be sitting there thinking, "Where the heck is Romans and what the heck is a Habakkuk?" All around me were these happy, diverse people who knew just what to do and exactly what was going on. They were all different ages and they carried themselves so much differently than my crew.

It was like when Ace Ventura was at the Cannibal Corpse concert. He was walking around knowing he didn't fit in. All these metalheads dressed in black with long hair were moshing on the dance floor, and he had his Hawaiian shirt open with a tucked-in white tank top underneath. But even though he was completely out of place, he still walked through the front door, started talking to people in the mosh pit, and ended up finding what he was looking for. My experience was the opposite. The church people were the ones colorfully dressed. I was in a black T-shirt, black jeans, and black Vans. But like Ace Ventura, I went in knowing that this was the place I would find what I was looking for.

Who was I now that I identified as a Christian? I knew that I was just a sinner saved by grace, same as all these other people in the church. I also knew that a church was supposed to be like a spiritual hospital where spiritually sick people could come to get well. That was me, so I knew that I was in the right place.

I was facing an identity crisis. Was it okay to still be me—you know, just a cleaned-up version of the knucklehead I was? And what would a cleaned-up version of me look like? Did it mean that I'd have to start changing the way I dressed and talked so that I'd fit in? Most importantly, what did God want from me? What changes was He expecting? Figuring out who you are once you become a Christian is one of the most important issues a new believer in Jesus has to deal with. I've seen too many people who couldn't answer this question crash and burn a few months into their faith.

Quick break again: all sorts of people call themselves Christians, but a lot of them use the word quite differently. Some think they are Christians because their parents call themselves Christians. Others believe they are Christians because they live in a "Christian" country. Still more think they are Christians by the process of elimination—"I'm not a Buddhist or a Hindu or a Muslim, so I must be a Christian."

But there is only one real definition for being a Christian. A Christian is someone who has received Jesus as their Savior and Lord and now has the Holy Spirit inside of them. What this means is that you have trusted that Jesus is the only One who can forgive your sins (remember, sins are all the bad things that we do to hurt ourselves and others and that go against God). He can do this because He died on the cross for us. That sacrifice of Himself was enough to wipe out our sins once and for all. So you ask for His forgiveness and He becomes your Savior. Then you make a promise—a commitment—to Him that you will do your best to live the way He wants you to live. That's how you make Him your Lord—the One that you will follow throughout your life. He's now the Lord over you and all you do. But don't worry—God's not uptight. He wants you to have a good time. He just doesn't want you to ruin your life by doing something stupid. So relax—Him being Lord over your life is a great thing. Trust me! Becoming a Christian is not complicated. It's all about having a relationship with Jesus and following Him.

That's the forgiveness I received from Jesus as my Savior and the commitment I made to Him as my Lord. That's what changed me top to bottom. The question I had to figure out was "Now what?" In this chapter, I'm going to show you how God took me from absolute confusion to absolute contentment in who He created me to be.

———————————

The day after I got back from Panama, I met with my brother at C1RCA. I told him I had a drug problem and he was amazingly supportive. He just wanted me to get healthy. So, we decided that it was best for me to take a year to get clean and to get my head screwed on straight so I could get my life figured out. After that time I'd come back on board and do marketing from the office. An office gig would keep me from traveling and getting into those places where I was partying every night.

Next stop after C1RCA was my dad's church. I needed to talk to my dad and I also needed to get a new Bible. I had left the King James Bible I stole from the hotel back on the plane. I got to the church and went upstairs to my dad's office. I told him, "All right, Dad, I need to figure out what I should do next." I was thinking that I needed to get myself into a rehab, because that's just what people did. So, I was checking out places like Teen Challenge and U-Turn for Christ. Those are great faith-based programs, but my dad knew me and he knew what it was that I needed. He said to me, "Ryan, what you need to do is read your Bible." Then he loaded me up with CDs of *Through the*

Bible by Pastor Chuck Smith. It would have been so much easier if The Word for Today (TWFT) app had been available back then. You know what? Those words from my dad were the best advice anyone's ever given me!

Don't get me wrong—I'm not knocking rehabs. I'm no Amy Winehouse—no, no, no. In fact, once The Whosoevers got started, a lot of my early ministry was done in rehabs. But my dad knew me. He knew that I am an all-or-nothing guy. If I was going to dive into the Bible, I was going to dive in deep. And that's just what I did.

But to dive into the Bible, I first needed a Bible. I walked down to the church bookstore and told them I had sucked at school. I let them know about my poor reading level and my ADD and how I needed a Bible that has a simple translation that I could understand. They led me to the New Living Translation (NLT). I pulled one off the shelf and was walking to the counter to pay for it when I looked to the right and saw this book that caught my eye. It was called *Save Me from Myself,* and on the cover was this sketchy-looking guy with long hair and covered with tattoos all over his body. I'm like, "Who is this dude? He looks like he could be one of my homies. What's he doing in a Christian bookstore?"

I grabbed the book and I asked, "Who's this?" The person at the counter said, "That's Brian 'Head' Welch, the guitar player from Korn. He's a Christian now." I was like, "No way. That's sick!" I didn't grow up listening to Korn, but I knew who they were. There was one song of theirs that I remembered seeing on MTV that I really liked—but if you see Head, don't tell him; he still thinks that I never listened to their stuff back then. Korn is one of the biggest bands on the planet, so I couldn't believe that this guy, Brian Welch, was actually a believer in Christ. At that moment I experienced this huge feeling of relief. I was standing in this church and I felt like a black sheep—like I didn't fit the mold or like I didn't really belong. But then I saw this dude who looked like my squad, and he's a Christian. It was a big moment. It fired me up to keep moving forward in my relationship with Jesus Christ.

I bought the Bible and I also got Head's book, and when I made it home, I started reading. I couldn't put his book down. Even with how badly I read, I still finished the thing in something like three days. I could relate to everything that he was going through—the bad relationships and the drugs and the anger. I remember thinking, "If I ever write a book, my book would be like this." When I finished it, this crazy thing happened. Even though I had never met Head before in my life—I didn't even have any connection to him or to Korn or to anyone in that camp—I felt this powerful intuition that I was going to work with him someday. It wasn't just a thought or a wish— it was closer to an "I know this is going to happen." I think that was probably the second time in my life that the Holy Spirit spoke to me—the first being that kids' song with the lyrics "This is the day the Lord has made..." Already God was preparing me for what He had ahead.

———————

Exactly as my dad predicted, I jumped all in to the Bible. I was reading it every day. I was listening to Bible studies. I was hitting up church six to seven days a week. Seriously, I was literally scouting out where they were doing church services around my house. Monday nights I went to a study at Calvary Chapel with Garid Beeler. Tuesday nights I was with a bunch of old people at Costa Mesa. Let me tell you, even though they all were sporting beehives, they were all very loving and accepting! Wednesday nights were for a Bible study at my dad's church; then I hit up another church on Thursdays. I tracked down some more churches that held Friday and Saturday studies. I was stalking churches for Bible studies. I wanted to learn and grow fast in the "faith [that] comes from hearing, that is, hearing the Good News about Christ" (Romans 10:17). So any place where they were digging into the Bible, I was there. It was my mission to grow in knowledge fast.

This became my rehab. When I prayed, God took away the desires for the drugs and the alcohol overnight. But I still needed to get myself strong, because those temptations could come back at any time. The kind of strength I needed could only come from the Word of God and the power of the Holy Spirit working in my life. Remember those verses we looked at a couple of chapters ago from 2 Timothy? "All Scripture is inspired by God and is useful to teach us what is true and to make us realize what is wrong in our lives. It corrects us when we are wrong and teaches us to do what is right. God uses it to prepare and equip his people to do every good work" (3:16–17). The Bible isn't just some history book or list of rules. It is like a spiritual boot camp. When we read it, it builds up our muscles until we get spiritually ripped and we're prepared for war. We become like biblical Spartans from the *300* movie. The Bible makes us strong enough to say no to the desires of the flesh when they come creeping back in to take us down. It's in the Bible that we learn what's right and wrong so we're prepared to do what God wants us to do. Then He can use our life in a powerful way, and that's what it's all about.

One of the things you learn by reading the Bible is how easy it actually is to not do the wrong stuff. Jesus boils it all down to two things—love God and love others, just like we read in the last chapter. When we are doing what God wouldn't want us to do or when we are hurting others, then that's sin. Stop it! But when we are doing things that show love to God and other people, then that's the good stuff.

If I was going to do right and keep away from the wrong, then I had to get strong fast, because I was still hanging out with my friends. They hadn't gone through the same change I had, so they were still smoking weed and drinking. And even though I wasn't feeling tempted to go back to those particular things, there were others that were much harder to say no to. There were girls wherever I would go. A lot of those girls were single and ready to mingle, and obviously I still liked the idea of hooking up with girls—duh. But I knew it wasn't right— God created sex for marriage. More and more often, when I'd be hanging out, the Holy Spirit would be telling me, "Dude, you can't be here this long." That was part of God renewing my mind. He knew that if I would post up long enough, I would give in sooner or later—it was just a matter of time. It used to be that all I wanted to do was hang out at parties, but now I found myself just getting bored. The conversations—the vibe—they just weren't doing it for me anymore. There had been a change in my mindset.

The life of getting wasted and high is all so shallow. Way back when, I'd spend the whole evening chasing girls, and depending on how drunk I would get, pretty much anything

could happen—a fight, jail, a DUI, or a three-day bender in Las
Vegas; all of those happened at least once. But when I was with
Christians, I noticed it was totally different. We were talking
about what God was doing in our lives because awesome stuff
was happening every single day. I wanted to talk about life and
my future and goals, not all the dead things that mean absolutely nothing. When I was at those parties, it was like I was in
the desert. It was all heat and sun and I'm thirsty and everything
around me is dead—drugs, booze, sex—deadness as far as the
eye can see. But when I was in a conversation with Spirit-filled
Christians, I'd be talking about God and the things of God and
what God was doing in my life and in their lives. Instead of a
desert, it was like being in a tropical paradise, where there's fruit
hanging from the trees and the water is warm—there are water-
falls and colorful birds and friendly monkeys. You just want to
chill there forever. One week every September, my brother had
the island of Tavarua in Fiji on lockdown. It was perfect condi-
tions and we'd have the whole island and the surf spots all to
ourselves. Yeah, it was just way better.

When you're digging into the Bible and the Word of God
comes alive for you and the torrents of living water that Jesus
talks about are bubbling up inside of you, that's when you find
joy in your life. That's when life gets epic. The living water adds
freshness to your life and you start producing fruit. These are
things done for God that help change the lives of the people
around you. Still not sure what this fruit is that I'm talking
about? Let me break it down a little more.

Let's say you plant an apple tree in your backyard. What are
you expecting to grow on it? Apples. Are you going to have to
teach it to produce apples? Are you going to have it go through

apple-making school? Of course not. An apple tree grows apples—that's just what it does. Another question: Are you going to have to go out and try to convince it to grow apples? "Come on, apple tree. Please squeeze out an apple for me. I know you can do it. Just push real hard." Again, no. Fruit trees produce fruit—it's as natural as natural can be. In fact, there are only two things that can go wrong—either the tree can go bad or it doesn't get taken care of properly. If a worm gets in the tree or it gets diseased, the fruit can go bad. A bad tree produces bad fruit. Or, if you neglect the tree—not watering it or pruning it—the tree will die. Dead trees don't produce dead fruit; they produce no fruit.

The Bible compares us to fruit trees. Fruit will naturally grow in us. We don't have to coax it out—it just happens. This "fruit" is how we live. It is our actions. It's how we treat people. It's our attitudes and behaviors. It's the great stuff we do for God and the bad stuff we do for ourselves. The goodness or badness of our fruit depends on us—the trees. If we belong to God and are spending time in the Bible and in prayer and are following the Holy Spirit, we are going to be cranking out some seriously juicy fruit. "But the Holy Spirit produces this kind of fruit in our lives: love, joy, peace, patience, kindness, goodness, faithfulness, gentleness, and self-control" (Galatians 5:22–23). But just before this good list is a bad list—the nasty fruit we'll produce if we don't take care of the tree. "Now the works of the flesh are evident: sexual immorality, impurity, sensuality, idolatry, sorcery, enmity, strife, jealousy, fits of anger, rivalries, dissensions, divisions, envy, drunkenness, orgies, and things like these" (Galatians 5:19–21 ESV). This happens when we don't water our tree with the Word of God and with prayer and with the Holy

Spirit. The tree becomes worthless—only good to be cut down and burned.

———————

So, when we're following the Holy Spirit, life will be epic and full of spiritual fruit. But what does that look like? To be this good, healthy, fruit-growing tree, do I have to totally change who I am and become a slacks-and-button-up-sporting, comb-over-wearing Christian? Is that what God wants us to look like? I want you to read this next statement very carefully: One of the greatest lies that the devil uses to drag away new believers from a legit relationship with Jesus is that when you give your life to God and start following Him, then you can't have any more fun and your life is going to suck. Dude, you're a Christian now? Awesome! Now toss all your favorite music, stop skating and surfing, and don't talk to any of your friends—become a weirdo and forget going to concerts and doing anything else you might enjoy doing, and would you please get a freaking haircut already? You end up comparing yourself to everyone else around you, and you start feeling like you can never measure up. That is such a big lie. God created us to have fun! Otherwise, He would have made everything boring. Life would be totally lame. But people buy into the lie. They're like, "My life sucks now that I'm a Christian, because all I do is go to church and then come home." I'm thinking, "Yeah, if that's your life, then it does suck! I wouldn't want to live your life, either."

I'm not saying that you don't change or that you don't need to uproot some of the old junk out of your new life. If there are parts of the way you live that are against God, then you need to cut them out. If the music you are listening to is sexualized and is talking about drugs and is filled with a ton of cuss words, it's going to lead your mind to places it shouldn't go. Stop listening to it. If you are wearing clothes that are designed to get the guys around you all hot and bothered, then stop wearing them. Besides, if those are the kind of guys you're looking to attract, then your standards are extremely low. Jesus said that what you put into your body is what comes out. So, if the stuff you are putting into your brain is garbage, then garbage is what will come out. But—and listen to me here—not every mainstream or secular band is putting garbage in. You don't have to be one of those uptight, judgmental Christians who think that everything that's not cranked out by the church factory is evil. Just because a song isn't written by a well-known Christian artist doesn't mean that it's of the devil. I know a lot of non-Christian artists that write some pretty amazing music.

This is all part of that new believer identity crisis. The lie of the devil is that you have to be isolated in the institution of the church—if that were true, then it would be lame. Let's be honest: the church hasn't been pushing out the most creative entertainment. So much of it is unbelievably cheesy. Christianity seems to run about ten years behind what is happening in culture. A lot of this is the fault of the Christian industry. The church has become cornball and goofy, and the unchurched know it. If you put out anything really creative or up to par with the rest of culture, then you are labeled as "of the world." But if you put out anything acceptable to the institutional church, then—like my daughters would say, "Ta-da!!"—you find yourself outdated to the culture. The devil's judgmental lies are making the Christian industry socially behind—creatively out of date. The church can't reach culture, because they aren't even operating in the right decade.

If you don't fit into the institutional church, then where do you fit in? And, more importantly, how do you know if how you want to live your life is cool with God or if you're crossing a line? That's why you get into the Bible. That's why you pray and ask the Holy Spirit to show you what's up. It's not up to the church and its traditions to tell you what's good and what's bad. Don't get me wrong—there are a lot of good churches out there that can give you some great wisdom based directly on the Word of God. But if someone can't back up chapter and verse the rules he's feeding to you, then don't give him the time of day. God is the One who has set our standards, and the Holy Spirit is the One who will keep you in check. That's why we call it a "personal" relationship.

I used to have a picture of Jimi Hendrix hanging on the wall of my living room. It was a beautiful chalk drawing that a friend of mine made specially for me. Jimi's got this big Afro and he's got a joint hanging out of his mouth. It was done with black chalk on white canvas. It was epic—one of the sickest pieces of art I've ever seen. Then one day I walked in after hearing a study on getting rid of the things that hinder your relationship with God. I looked at this piece of chalk art, and it just didn't feel right anymore. It wasn't making me want to smoke weed or anything, and it's not like I was sinning by having it. In fact, I totally loved the piece and it lit up my living room. But something had changed—the Holy Spirit had moved. I said, "You know what, God? I'm going to offer this to You as a sacrifice. I'm going to give this to You even though I love it with all my mind, body, and soul. It's Yours now, because I want to show You that even more than I love this picture, I love You with all my mind, body, and soul. I don't want anything to hinder my relationship with You or Your plans for my life." I lifted it off the wall, took it to the garage, and put it in the trash. I didn't give it to anyone else, because I didn't want someone else to possibly be tempted or inspired to smoke weed. I just took it out and dumped it, because I felt like that's what God wanted me to do. That, my friends, is the way the Holy Spirit works. This only happens when you're in step with God's Spirit. But if you continue to put garbage in, you will continue to have garbage come out. You will never hear the Holy Spirit talking to you.

One day, Jesus was choppin' it up with His crew and said, "If any of you wants to be my follower, you must give up your own way, take up your cross, and follow me" (Mark 8:34). When I first read that verse, it became a pivotal point in my life, and suddenly, there I was at the crossroads again. I've come to realize that in the Christian journey, you will find yourself at the crossroads often. It's those moments when God is moving, and He is watching to see what road you're going to choose to take. Will it be your will or His will?

It was early on in my all-or-nothing Bible study period, and it wasn't like people were coming up to me saying, "Hey, Ryan, you've got to get rid of the cigarettes and the porn and the cussing or that's it for you." Instead, it was simply me saying to God, "I'm Yours. I'm picking up my cross. I'm following You." After I told Him that, then through my times reading the Bible and praying and listening to God, the Holy Spirit started pointing out to me, one by one, the things that He wanted me to give up and to change. It was also during these times that He showed me all the music that was still cool for me to listen to and what concerts I could still go to.

God started doing these little shifts in my life because I was open. "God, what do You want to do in me today? What do You want me to remove? What do You want me to add?" He was leading me, impressing on my heart and thoughts, showing me exactly who He wanted me to be. The Spirit was helping me remove all the hang-ups I had about people and about life. That's how God took the lead in my whole cleanup process. And that's how He began giving me back my identity in Him.

During that time of personal overhaul and reboot, I started looking for Christian guys I could hang out with—other men who were like-minded. This is key to not getting discouraged. If you don't hang out with people that are like-minded, you're going to get frustrated and bored. Pray about it, and God will send them your way in His time.

That's when I started spending a lot of time with Sonny Sandoval, the lead singer for P.O.D. I had met Sonny years prior through Michael Guido. Michael's a Christian guy who goes on tours with traveling bands, discipling them on the road and pouring into their lives. One day before I got right with God, he called my cell when I was in my office at C1RCA and caught me on one of the rare days I was actually in the country. He said, "Hey, me and Sonny are here in San Clemente, if you're around." I said, "Yeah, dude, bring him by." Later, I hooked Sonny up with some product, because that was part of my job—getting artists repping C1RCA gear. P.O.D. was massive, and besides that, Sonny was a believer and was really cool and down-to-earth.

The first week after I came back from Panama, I made a call to Sonny. I told him, "Hey, man, I'm reaching out to you to let you know that I'm taking a year off from C1RCA, and I'm just posting up at my dad's church right now trying to figure out what I want to do next. I hear my dad booked your band for a night at his crusade. I'm going to be working on the Saturday-night event. It will be good to connect."

Quick backstory: My dad used to put on a music festival in the '80s called Exit Festival. He'd have a big lineup of bands, mostly punk rock and new wave—Christian artists who were actually relevant at that time and on point. They'd play, then my dad would speak, and you'd see a whole bunch of people giving their lives to God.

Right after I told my dad that Jesus had gotten hold of my life, he told me about this big three-day crusade he had coming up in downtown LA. The final night was going to be youth oriented, so he had booked P.O.D. to perform. Knowing my history with producing events and my friendship with Sonny, my dad asked me if I wanted the keys to Saturday night. I jumped at the chance.

Remembering his old Exit festivals, I used the Exit name to rebrand that final night of the crusade—relaunching it for the twenty-first century. I connected with one of my artist friends from LA, and we came up with a whole new fresh campaign for this Saturday-night event. We were marketing to the masses. We did mainstream radio ads. We restructured the whole format so it was like going to a real concert. It was during this time that Sonny and I really connected back up.

When it came off, it was awesome. The music was rocking, the Gospel was clear, and people got saved. That night began a series of Exit festivals. In 2009, we hit Vegas with the Exit Lost Vegas festival, which we tied in with this crazy art campaign and had eighteen thousand people show up. Then in 2010, we held Exit One Love for Chi—a fundraising concert for Chi Cheng of the Deftones, who had been in a coma after a major car wreck in 2008. In between those events, we also put on a celebration for the US Marines down in SoCal, which saw twenty thousand coming through the gates at the Twentynine Palms base.

A little while after that first Exit concert, my dad told me about a trip the church was taking to Israel. He asked if some of my buddies and I wanted to come along. I have family who moved to Israel to become missionaries back in the 1960s. So I had been visiting the Holy Land since I was a kid, and I was excited to get back. I naturally thought of Sonny coming along, too. I called him up and said, "Dude, you want to go to Israel? I need a roommate." Sonny's like, "Yeah, I'll roll." A couple of our other friends went along, too, and it was incredible. We're cruising around on this tour seeing the places where Jesus walked, checking out the sites where so many of the Bible stories took place. It was so awesome.

Meanwhile, Sonny and I were really getting close, hanging out every day. He had some stuff going on in his life that he was processing through, too. He had just walked away from P.O.D. to take some time off. He felt he had kinda compromised on some things—nothing crazy—but now he wasn't really where he wanted to be with God. He was in a place where he was like, "Man, I got to get back on track and in step with God." Right before we left for Israel, he had shaved off his trademark dreads as a sign of renewal—an offering to God to show that he was all in.

As we were talking one day, Sonny was telling me about all these ideas he had. Remember what I said earlier about hanging out with like-minded people? That's how creativity and ideas combine to birth movements. At the same time, I was still trying to figure out what I was going to do with my life. I had helped my dad rebirth Exit, and it was a great feeling working on music festivals again. But I knew that the clock was ticking on C1RCA. Did God want me to go back when my year was up, or was He calling me to something new? I was open to doing what God wanted me to do. I just didn't know what that was.

That was when Sonny said, "Hey, man, I've got this idea— actually, it's really just a name. The Whosoevers. Originally, I was going to use it for a reggae band I was thinking of starting. But as I keep thinking about it, I'm really seeing it as more of a worldwide movement of people who believe in Jesus." He said, "As I'm traveling around the world, I've discovered that there are so many different kinds of Christianity. In Africa, they're all about their awesome worship. But that worship is so different from what you find in South and Central America. Then you've got something else going on in Russia and Europe, and then there's Asia and all their underground churches. But we're all united together in one incredible family of God."

When Sonny said "different kinds of Christianity," he wasn't talking about different belief systems. We're all sinners saved by grace—all washed clean by faith in the blood of Jesus Christ. He was referring to believers who love God and whose theology is sound but who are all doing church their way. Some worship with a full band, some just use drums, some don't use any instruments at all. It just depends on the culture. So, Sonny was talking about breaking through the cultures of Christianity and being united in Christ to reach the world for God. You know the Great Commission? If you don't, don't sweat it—you'll hear about it plenty in chapters to come.

As Sonny was talking, I was getting more and more fired up. I was seeing the vision of what he was talking about. I could see his words in my mind and all that this movement could become. If you ever get the opportunity to meet Sonny, you'll realize that he's the real deal. He loves God with all his heart. He said to me, "If we can just all come together in unity with the Gospel of Jesus Christ to let people know that Jesus loves them, we can reach the world. Then all these new Whosoevers—all those who believe in Jesus Christ and ask Him into their hearts just like John 3:16 talks about—all of us can come together for the cause of spreading the Gospel. That's what I see for The Whosoevers Movement."

As I was listening to Sonny, my soul said, "That's it!" I saw the vision, clear as day. I told him, "Dude, that's sick! I'm down. I can help you put that together. I'll help you with marketing and design. Let's start with the logo concept. Let's get it going, man. I'll do my part and God will do His part, and this thing is going to blow up."

We kept talking about The Whosoevers through the rest of the trip. Then when we were just about at the end, we visited the

Garden of Gethsemane. We all gathered around and a pastor stood up to give us a message about what had gone down in that garden.

He said, "This is where Jesus was the night before He was going to be crucified. This was going to be the most important event in the history of the world. Jesus was about to die on the cross and take all the sins of the world upon Himself. With His death on that cross, He was going to defeat Satan. Three days later He would rise up from the dead, and, not long after, ascend up to heaven to prepare a place so that everyone who believes in Him can live with Him forever. It's the blood that would be shed on that cross that will wash each of us white as snow, if we'll just trust Him. Then once His blood purifies us, Jesus sends the Holy Spirit. He's the One who is the power that allows us to live a Spirit-led life." I was sitting there thinking, "This guy just perfectly described a Whosoever—a follower of Christ." "For God so loved the world that He gave His only begotten Son, that whosoever believes in Him should not perish but have everlasting life" (John 3:16).

Then the pastor looked over to our group and said, "All you guys who have come from LA and other places on planet Earth to meet us here—a lot of you have come with baggage. All your lives, you've been saying in your hearts, 'My will be done, my will be done.' You've brought all this 'me first' baggage sixteen hours across the seas to Israel, and my question is, are you going to fly that same baggage all the way back home? Are you going to go back to your same lives, saying, 'My will be done'? Or are you going to say what Jesus said in this garden, 'Father, not My will, but Yours be done'? The next day, Jesus went to the cross.

He was all in following the will of the Father. Now you have a choice to make. Are you going to go back to LA and live the same life of chaos and unrest or are you going to say to God, 'Not my will, but Your will be done'?"

Man, that hit me so hard. I needed some time to process what the pastor had just said and what was going on in my heart and mind. Deep down I knew the answer, because it was burning inside of me. So, what came next was perfect timing. He told us to go spend some time on our own. We all scattered around the garden and I remember just dropping down in the dirt. I knew I was at a crossroads. This was the moment of truth—was I all in or not? My heart was pounding. I was excited and nervous at the same time. With everything in my heart and my mind and my soul I prayed, "God, I will do whatever You want me to do. You ask, and I'm in." Then I kept going and said something that I'm not even sure where it came from. I said, "And, Jesus, if You want me to tell my story—even though I don't want to—if it's Your will for me to tell it, then I will. I don't care anymore— I won't keep hiding my story."

You've got to realize what a big deal this was for me. You wouldn't know it by how often I'm now speaking to huge crowds, but I was terrified to talk in front of a group of people. Prior to this I'd been hit up by my dad saying, "Hey, Ryan, you should give your testimony." And I'm like, "You're tripping!" Seriously, when we got back from Israel, they wanted us to get up onstage in front of the church and tell everyone about our trip. We were all lined up backstage ready to go on. Right when the music ended and we were supposed to walk out, I turned and broke out the side door. Dude, true story—that's how scared I was to go onstage at church and talk in front of people.

So, I prayed this prayer, but I gave God an impossible condition. I told Him, "If You want me to tell my story, I will—one hundred percent. But just so I know it's from You, You've got to have someone ask me that's not in my inner circle. I don't want my dad. I don't want one of my friends. I want someone totally not connected to me to contact me and invite me to tell my story. Lord, my life is Yours from this point on. I'll do whatever You want me to do—I'll go wherever You want me to go. Forget the music and skate industry"—that was a tough one, because that was my life's passion, but I was laying it all down for Him—"forget everything else. I just want to follow You. But if You want me to tell my story—if that's part of it—then have someone contact me."

Even today, I have a hard time keeping back the emotions thinking about that time in the garden, sitting there in the dirt. I was so sincere with God—so real. And that's basically the essence of our relationship with Him. Complete surrender and being real with Him—that's our heart posture; that's true worship. All or nothing. That's what God is looking for from us. Are you in or are you out? I was telling God, "Okay, Lord, I'm all in. Let's go!" So, that's my question for you—are you in or are you out? Everything rides on your answer.

The next day, while I was still in Israel, I got a call. It was from a pastor from Calvary Chapel Spring Valley. I'm standing there wondering why this dude I had met only once before at some pastors' meeting was ringing me up all the way over in Israel. He said, "Hey, Ryan, I want you to come tell your story at my church." I was in shock. I managed to say, "Yeah, man, I will." Inside, though, I was thinking, "I can't believe what just happened." God was proving that not only is He real, but He also likes to drop surprises on His kids every now and then.

I tracked down Sonny and told him, "You are not going to believe this. I said this prayer in the Garden of Gethsemane yesterday and today I get a call from a pastor in Vegas asking me to come tell my story. This is crazy." Sonny starts laughing and says, "No way!" Then I said, "Dude, you've got to come with me. I'm scared."

Sonny said, "Don't worry—I'll roll out with you. I'm with you, man." That's just one of the reasons Sonny's so dope.

We got back home from Israel and the time came when we were about to head to Vegas. Sonny and I were hanging out in Diamond Bar, and I said to him, "Look, next week is when I'm telling my story. Would you call Head and ask him to come out? I read his book and I'd really like to meet him. Maybe we could all just kick back in Vegas for a night."

Sonny and Head went way back. When Head gave his life to God, the first person that he called before he went public on MTV was Sonny. He knew that Sonny was a Christian, and he wanted to talk through his next steps. Sonny told him, "Dude, just chill. Love God—figure out who He is and then come out later to the world. Get yourself solid, because when you make your worldwide statement, everyone—Christians and non-Christians—is going to attack and judge you." Head didn't listen and came out with a bang, and when you're through with this book, you can read his book and hear his story.

Sonny called Head, told him about me, and asked him to come. Head's like, "Yeah, man, I'll fly out and meet you guys."

Then I called Lacey Sturm, lead singer of Flyleaf at that time, and invited her. I knew that she was a Christian from when Michael Guido introduced me a few months back. Also, Sonny had done a song with her at the New Year's Eve Times Square event in New York City. So everyone ended up meeting for dinner at P.F. Chang's in Vegas.

It took only a few minutes before we all felt like we knew each other really well. We realized we were all the same. We loved God with all of our hearts, even though we were still a little rough around the edges. We were just looking for ways to serve God and get the Gospel out. Again, it is such an amazing thing to be around believers who are like-minded. Everyone just wanted to love each other and love God. There was no pride at the table—no ego. These guys and this girl had all sold millions of albums—if there was ever a place where there could be pride and ego or some weird "it's all about me" vibe, that table would have been it. Seriously, I have been around plenty of church leaders who think they're rock stars or too cool for school and have felt that vibe. But around this table, there was none of it. Just people whose hearts were absolutely open and transparent—what you see is what you get. When you put servants together who are sold-out with no ego, you can change the world. And we were getting ready to try.

At the end of our conversation, I said, "Hey, guys, I'm supposed to tell my testimony tomorrow. But forget it—let's all go and tell our testimonies." So, the next morning, we went up together. We told our stories and we saw all kinds of people get saved. A cool bonus was that my dad, who had tried to get me to tell my story before, was there with his best friend, Dale. It was the first time he saw me give my testimony—that was special.

That morning was the birth of The Whosoevers Movement. We weren't even calling it The Whosoevers Movement yet, but that was the moment. It just happened. It was all God working through hearts surrendered to Him. And it all began back in the Garden of Gethsemane in the dirt among a bunch of knotted, old olive trees. I was broken and done with my old life. I had no idea that the simple prayer of obedience I prayed that day— "God, my life is Yours. No matter where You take me, I'm just going to follow You"—would launch into a worldwide movement that would see hundreds of thousands of people get saved in the years since we started back in 2009.

Peter and the disciples were out in a boat, trying to keep from drowning in a storm. Suddenly, they saw this silhouette coming across the water. The disciples were like, "Uh-oh! It's a ghost!"

But Peter took a second look. "Jesus, is that You?" he called out.

Jesus said, "Yeah, it's Me. I'm just out here chillin', walking on the water and stuff."

Squinting hard through the rain, Peter shouted, "Jesus, if that's really You, then tell me to come walking on the water to You."

"Okay, Pete, roll out."

At this point, Peter could have looked back at the other eleven terrified disciples and down at the whitecapping water and said, "On second thought, Jesus, not Your will, but my will be done. It's way too scary stepping out of this boat." Instead, he put one leg over the side of the boat, then the other, and then he jumped. And in that one simple act of obedience, Peter learned he could live the impossible. That's the way it is with us. That's what God did with me. That's what He'll do with you, too.

It's the same with anybody who prays that "I'm going to follow You, Jesus" prayer. I had no clue what God was going to do with me. But He had this unique call on my life that I had no idea about yet. God's got a unique call on your life, too. God said, "For I know the plans I have for you…They are plans for good and not for disaster, to give you a future and a hope. In those days when you pray, I will listen. If you look for me wholeheartedly, you will find me" (Jeremiah 29:11–13). Think about that—God has a plan specifically for you. He created you specially so that you could get that plan done. You are not just an extra body in an overpopulated world—you are not just a face in the crowd to God. He has something unique and special set out for you, and you're going to lose your mind when you walk into it and realize what it is. You'll be getting up every morning saying, "I can't believe that I'm living this life!" Trust me—that's how I start each morning.

But that's only going to happen with full surrender to God. Without full surrender—without you saying, "Not my will, God, but Yours be done"—it's never going to happen. Be who God created you to be. Throw up your white flag! Live the surrendered life He's got planned out for you.

CHAPTER 6

Shiny Objects

Fish are not smart. Now, I know that half of you reading this are saying, "Dang, Ryan, thanks for the deep insight." The other half of you are like, "My tenth-grade biology teacher told me that dolphins are so smart that if they had opposable thumbs, they'd take over the world." I hear you, but, first of all, dolphins are not fish. Second of all, come on—they're just dolphins.

So, back to my original statement—fish are not smart. That's why if you give three kids each a rod with a hook and a worm, chances are when they drop the line off the end of a pier, one of them is going to end up reeling in some lunch. Fish is hungry. Fish sees food. Fish eats food. Fish becomes food.

Even though fish are not smart, some have a better technique for avoiding the sharp hook from lodging in their jaw.

There are fish that are cruising around when they come across a worm floating around in the water. Some God-given instinctual part of them says, "Wait, something here's not right. This whole scene is looking a bit sketchy. I've been swimming these waters for a while now, and I don't remember seeing any underwater worms before." So, they flip a U-turn and they're outskies.

Another fish may have ingrained in his tiny mind a time when he bit the worm and ended up getting pulled up out of the water. Then some guy painfully yanked the hook out of his mouth, took a selfie, then tossed him for a belly flop back into the water. So, when he sees the worm this time, his pea-sized brain fires off a flashback that says, "Not this time. I'm not going out like that."

It's these fish that you need to trick if they're going to end up as fish tacos. So, you pull a shiny lure from your tackle box—I'm talking next-level lure with a rainbow pattern and glitter—and attach it to your line. The fish that knows about the old worm trick is swimming along, and suddenly he sees something flashing at him. His fish brain says, "Dude, flash means food for whatever reason. Let's check it out." He swims over and sees the worm that got him before. But this time, the worm is flashing. Can't say no to flashing. It looks way too good to say no. He takes a bite and finds himself hooked in the jaw again and making another trip to the surface—fish-swearing all the way to the top.

Satan has a big fishing pole and he's got a huge tackle box full of the best lures in the business. All he needs to do is tie on his line one of those shiny objects specially designed to get our attention, cast it out, and we immediately start jumping at the bait. Most times it seems he barely needs to try because we're so easy.

But we don't have to bite. Even though we act sometimes like we've just got fish brains and we can't stop ourselves, we've really got so much more. We can flip a U-turn and swim the other way. We can just say no.

The Bible says to "resist the devil, and he will flee from you" (James 4:7). That word "resist" means to fight against something. It's a very strong word. If I have you pinned up against the wall and I'm trying to put my knife into your throat, I promise you that you're going to do everything in your power to stop me. It's life-or-death. That's the true meaning of resist. Now, go back and read that verse again and ask yourself whether you really resist sin and the devil. Or do you just let him stick it to you with no resistance? Remember, this is a battle we're talking about. How can we fight it and win? How do we turn away in the midst of temptation, and what are the shiny objects that we need to be watching out for?

When I came back from Panama, I got serious with God and started to read and study the Bible. God began cleaning me up with the living water. He was doing what's called a sanctification process, which is just another way of saying He's helping me get rid of all the bad junk from my life and filling it up instead with good stuff. Immediately when I first prayed for help, God healed me of the drugs and the alcohol. This was a major miracle. I liked the way beer tastes and the way drugs made me feel. That's the whole reason why people do them. So when God took those cravings away from me, it was huge and it was a total God thing. I can't take any credit for that—not one bit.

But that was just a first step. I wanted to get rid of everything that was keeping me from being as close as I could get with God—anything that would jeopardize my relationship with Him. I was going to church. I was reading my Bible and praying. Along with getting rid of the drugs and the drinking, I wasn't sleeping with girls anymore. I had even stopped almost all of my cussing, which was definitely a thing. I used to fire off the f-word at least three times per sentence. But God was dealing with that, too. So much good stuff was happening in my life—but I was still struggling with watching porn.

As I mentioned earlier, porn was my secret sin—my hidden indulgence. I could act out knowing there was no chance of getting caught. Nobody knew about it—all they saw was the new Ryan, the changed Ryan. They had no clue what was happening when I got back home. But God knew. He knows our heart and He sees everything. I felt convicted before God, and I knew it was messing with my relationship with Him. So, I finally got to the point where I was like, "Okay, forget this. I'm over it. I don't want to be a poser anymore." I didn't want to keep going back to pornography. I was tired of always feeling dirty and guilty afterward. I hate that.

I came to that verse in Mark that we talked about in the last chapter. Jesus tells the people who were hanging around Him, "If you want to be My disciples—My followers—you've got to turn from your selfish ways, pick up your cross, and follow Me." He's saying you've got to deny yourself and turn away from your body appetites. Doing that is going to cost something, just like Jesus dying on the cross cost Him something—His life. If I'm going to pick up my cross and follow Jesus, it's going to be tough and it's going to require sacrifice. In life, you can't accomplish anything great without sacrifice. Too many people are looking for the easy way and the shortcuts. There are no shortcuts to becoming a disciple. But even though it's hard work, we've got the Holy Spirit to help us along the way.

I decided that the Christian wannabe days were over. I was going to stop watching porn. I knew it wasn't what God wanted from me, and I was tired of feeling like a slave to it. I knew the damage that it does to people from the stories I'd heard and the statistics I'd read. I knew that it had already damaged my mind, and I was sick of the grip it had on me. I wanted to live the Gethsemane prayer of "not my will but Yours be done." So I prayed to God and said, "Okay, Lord, that's it. From this point on, I'm done."

It was another crossroads moment—a punk rock moment. I yelled out loud in my room, "God, that's it!" I was all pissed off because I knew what I was committing to and that it was going to suck! There are few things more enjoyable to a guy than checking out a hot girl. There's nothing that feels better than having sex with that hot girl you were checking out, right? Sex feels good—that's why people do it. If sex didn't feel so good, the human race would rapidly depopulate. For many guys and girls who don't have ready access to an actual person to have sex with, porn seems to them like a logical alternative. But for both sex outside of marriage and porn, there are side effects. Like we talked about in an earlier chapter, you reap what you sow. It's a cause-and-effect thing.

I didn't want anything in my life that could jeopardize the great changes that were going on in me. I wanted to sow good things so that I would reap good things. In other words, I wanted to live how God wanted me to live, not according to how my body appetites wanted to live. I knew that if I would get rid of the old ways and chase after the new ways, God would just keep making my life more epic. But that meant being 100 percent down for Him and not playing games. Too many people live at 5 percent or 10 percent for God—some even 50 or 60 percent—and then wonder why they aren't feeling God in their lives. It's like putting only one foot in a hot tub and wondering why your body is still shivering from the cold.

I prayed to God and told Him that I was done with the porn. I was tired of getting defeated by this giant. I was ready to go through the desert to reach the Promised Land, but I was going to need His help. And that prayer became a pattern for me. Every time I had those thoughts and desires to watch porn or go back to those things from my old life—and every time I still do—I prayed to God for help. And every time, He was there to step in. It was a supernatural work of the Lord. How else can you explain someone who has lived this life for so long and has been engaged in sex and porn and all these other things just quitting? It's not my willpower or my strength. It is the power of the Holy Spirit. He can help you quit just like He helped me quit. He can also keep you from going back.

I talk to so many people who say, "I stop for two weeks; then I go back." Or, "I stop for two months; then I go back." Or, "I stop for two years; then I go back." Dude, the desires never totally go away. But neither does the help of the Holy Spirit when we're following Him. The Bible says, "For I can do everything through Christ, who gives me strength" (Philippians 4:13). That means that Jesus Christ and His Spirit—the Holy Spirit—are there to give you the strength you don't have yourself.

God will give you the power to fight against temptation.

We, however, need to build up our resolve to turn to Him. We've been feeding our body appetites for so long they've gotten some serious muscle to them. We need to change our feeding habits. It's like having a couple of pit bulls. If you feed one and don't feed the other and then they get in a fight, the fed one is going to have power over the other. When it's strong enough, it will put the other one out of commission and the unfed one will die. This is the same with the flesh and the spirit. Whichever you feed will dominate. Before, I was feeding my flesh—those desires and appetites. If I was going to start living the way God wanted me to, I had to stop feeding my flesh pornography. Then it would start to die and begin to go away. In place of feeding my flesh, I had to start feeding my spirit the Word of God. Jesus called Himself the Bread of Life. When I fed on His words—the Bible—it took the food out of the mouth of the bad dog and put it into the mouth of the big dog.

If you're reading this thinking, "Dude, that's good for you, Ryan, but I suck as a Christian. Why can't I seem to just stop doing the wrong things as easily as you stopped?" If you think stopping all that stuff was easy, then you're not listening to what I'm saying. It was a day-after-day spiritual battle—a war between the flesh and the spirit that I didn't always win. The drugs and alcohol, God took away from me. The porn—that was a hard six-month struggle. But it wasn't even the biggest struggle I faced. The biggest battle for me? Quitting smoking. That was a serious fight.

Smoking was an integral part of my life. I had dabbled with

smoking since grammar school. Then I really got into it when I was fifteen. I had a habit every morning of grabbing a cigarette, lighting it, and putting it in my mouth. I'd hit it and get that burn in the back of my throat. I'd light up with my morning coffee and at the end of every meal—time after time every day. I liked smoking. I liked smoking weed. I liked smoking cigars. I liked smoking cigarettes. I loved the smell of pipe smoke. I really didn't want to stop.

On top of that, I wasn't ready to quit. This is true of a lot of people who are coming off drugs and alcohol. My thinking was, "Okay, I've given up so much other stuff; I can't give up cigarettes, too. That's too much." I think that if I had tried right when I got back from Panama, I would have just buckled. Besides, I knew it wasn't a sin to smoke cigarettes. I heard Chuck Smith say, "You won't go to hell for smoking—you'll just smell like hell and get to heaven faster." I knew that the Bible said that our bodies are temples of the Lord, so we shouldn't want to destroy them. We should treat them right and do our best to be healthy. I just didn't want to give those cigarettes up.

But I knew it was the right thing. Again, smoking is not treating our bodies properly. But more than that, God began moving in me—changing my attitude. The person of the Holy Spirit started to speak to me about quitting. I was beginning to feel conviction. I knew that it wasn't a good look—going someplace to talk about Jesus, then going outside to grab a smoke. Besides, I didn't want to be in bondage to anything. I didn't want to be anyone's or anything's slave. If you have to do something and you can't stop, you know what? You're a slave. I was tired of bowing down to the Marlboro Man. Besides, didn't the Marlboro Man die of lung cancer? Anyone who smokes knows their body is getting destroyed. They fill their lungs with smoke, they cough, they hack, then they take another drag.

This time, rather than it being an instantaneous freedom, it was another six-month-long process. I eventually gave up the cigarettes and moved to vaping, but the vaping still had me chained. During this time, I used to go on hikes in Laguna Hills. One day I was coming back to my car after listening to a Bible study, and I said to God, "You know what? I'm done with this." Yep, back at the crossroads. I said, "This is the last thing that I'm holding on to. It's the last habit that I haven't turned over to You. I want to be Your servant, not tobacco's slave." I went to my car and got my vaping machine out. I walked over to a trash can and dropped it in. I figured I needed to do it there in the hills for two reasons. The first reason was that when you read the Bible, God's people always made sacrifices in hills or high places—and believe me, this was a sacrifice. The second reason was more practical—I knew the cans would likely be emptied that night. If I had thrown them away at home, I probably would have dumpster-dove them back out of the trash later like nicotine slaves do. This way they were gone once and for all. Once I did this, there were no more cravings. It's as if God met me right at my crossroads. When I stepped out in faith to quit and I surrendered the habit to Him, He showed up and that was that—it was a wrap.

Living right with God is not an easy choice by any means. This is particularly true when you first start your relationship with Him, because you haven't known Him long enough to build up a lot of trust in Him. But the more you see Him come through, the easier it is to trust Him. You learn that He will never let you down or leave you hanging. He will be there for you without fail. When you start to really trust Him, Satan will come at you hard. The last thing he wants is another sold-out, committed believer. But you've got God on your side, who is always ready to give the devil a whupping. There are also steps you can take to build up your ability to say yes to God and no to the appetites of the body.

GET RID OF THE SIN OPPORTUNITIES

In the Bible, there's a story about a guy named Joseph. His life lately hadn't quite been going as planned. He grew up having it good. He was his dad's favorite, a fact he didn't mind occasionally rubbing in the faces of his ten older brothers. One day his pops called him over and said, "Joe, I sent your brothers out a few weeks ago to feed our sheep. I want you to go check on them and see how they're doing." So, Joseph took off to hunt down his brothers.

When he finally found them, they decided that this was their chance to get rid of Daddy's little pet. They grabbed hold of him, tied him up, and sold him to a passing caravan that was heading down to Egypt. Once he got there, Joseph was sold to a big-time government official named Potiphar. Through it all, Joseph stayed tight with God, and God blessed him as a result. Everything Joseph did succeeded—it was like everything he touched turned to gold. Potiphar saw this and soon Joseph was running the guy's whole house.

Too bad for Potiphar, his wife was scandalous. She saw this handsome young buck and she wanted him bad. Every chance she got, she tried to get Joseph into bed—giving him the eye and walking like an Egyptian. One day, Potiphar was off at work and wifey was chilling by the pool. She saw Joseph walking by and she couldn't take it anymore. Just like that, she attacked. She was kissing and grabbing and dragging and groping, and he was doing his best to fight her off. Finally, he broke free and she was left holding the clothes she had torn off of him. She screamed, said that Joseph had attacked her, and he ended up in an Egyptian prison.

Why did Joseph fight her off? If he had given in and hooked up with her, he probably could have gotten away with it. No one would have known. But he wanted to stay right with God. Joseph didn't want to offend his Lord and he knew that God would have seen. But more important to our discussion than why Joseph fought her off is how Joseph fought her off. He broke out of her grip and bolted out the door—fast as he could.

Paul the apostle wrote to his young protégé, Timothy, about all the temptations that people give in to. He then said, "But you, Timothy, are a man of God; so run from all these evil things" (1 Timothy 6:11). He's telling him, "Hey, Timothy, when you start feeling the pull of these body appetites that are trying to get a hook in you and take you down, remember that God gave you two feet—use them." That's how I'm able to battle the cravings for pornography and other sins. When I get those desires, I pray. Then I get myself away from the phone or the computer screen or whatever else is trying to drag me down. I run away from the unsafe zone to a place where the temptation can't follow me.

One night, a guy came up to me after I was done speaking. He said, "Hey, I want to stop porn. Tell me how I can quit." I asked him, "So where do you watch it?" He said, "I watch it on my computer at home." I told him, "Well, then get rid of your computer or get rid of your Wi-Fi." The dude was like, "What?" He just looked at me dumbfounded—like I had told him to empty his bank account into mine. For real, the face he gave me was classic! I said, "Don't you want to quit? If you do, you've got to run away from what's dragging you down." Remember, holiness is a battle. How hard are you willing to fight?

If you have a problem with alcohol but you keep hanging out with your friends at the bar, you're going to keep drinking. You can't put yourself in that scenario if you want to quit. Same is true for the porn. How much do you want to quit? How much are you willing to sacrifice for holiness? You may wonder why holiness is so important. Holiness is where the power of God comes from. The Bible says, "For if you live by [your sinful nature's] dictates, you will die. But if through the power of the Spirit you put to death the deeds of your sinful nature, you will live" (Romans 8:13). Putting something to death is a painful process.

If you want to quit doing the wrong things, it's going to hurt. The pain won't usually be physical, although sometimes if you're trying to get off drugs, you're going to face some necessary days of hell. Typically, the pain for holiness is tied to what you have to sacrifice. You may not be able to have Wi-Fi on your phone or at your house. Maybe you need to get a flip phone— you know, a dumb phone. You may need to put a blocker or an app on your phone and computer that limits what content will be allowed on it. I've suggested that to people, but they say, "Yeah, but those blockers aren't that good. They're always blocking out stuff that's not even close to pornographic. It's a pain in the butt." My answer is "It may be a pain in the butt, but how well is the other way working for you? Not so good, right? Sorry, dude, it's not going to be easy."

The problem is that people don't really want to quit. They prefer just to talk about how they have a problem and how hard it is to say no. They throw out a bunch of excuses so they can make themselves feel good while never dealing with the problem. Listen, man, are you telling me that you just can't stop having sex with your screen every time it comes on? Well, I guarantee you that if you have a porn problem, and you get rid of the internet on your phone and on your computer at your house, 100 percent you will not be watching porn. As funny and stupid as that sounds, it's the truth. So, if you're reading this book and you want to get rid of a porn problem, put the book down and get rid of your internet. Now. I'll wait…

It all goes back to the shiny objects. Satan is just dying to drop a sparkling new lure in front of you to see if you'll bite. You've got to limit his ability to hook you and reel you in. You've also got to be on the lookout, because he'll drop in the shiny objects even when you're not looking. I saw this happen in church with a guy I know. This new girl came in and she was the Barbie doll type. She was a new Christian and was carrying herself in an "I'm single and ready to mingle" kind of way, with tight clothes that accent just the right areas to make men look. This dude sees her and knows that he could never pull her in his wildest dreams. But here in church he's got a chance. She starts paying him attention, and the next thing you know they're in the sack together. Before, he had been helping out in a ministry—God was doing something awesome with him. But he got taken out just like that and he is no longer around. He got caught up and hooked.

These shiny objects can be a lot of things. I've just been focusing on porn because it is such a major issue for men and women inside and outside of the church. For you it could be a job that has you working so hard that you don't have time for your family and you can't manage to get yourself to church. For others it could be a relationship with someone who is not into God. Maybe that person is pulling you away from God and from reading the Bible. Sports, video games, and hobbies can grab hold of you and keep you away from what's really important. I'm not saying that you can't love to be out skating or surfing or shooting guns or whatever you're into. But if any of those things starts pulling you away from your relationship with God, then it becomes a problem. That's Satan's whole goal. He studies us. He's on the prowl. He's looking for a way to creep into your life. When we see him dropping the lure in, we've got to swim away with all we've got. That's resisting. Sometimes you fight by punching in the face and sometimes you fight by running away as fast as you can.

GET ACCOUNTABILITY

There's no reason to fight the good fight alone. You've got the person of the Holy Spirit with you giving you the strength to say no. But God also puts people around you who can take the holiness journey with you. Like I said earlier, if you struggle with porn, put all the blocks on your phone and get rid of the internet. But also tell someone about it. You're not a weirdo if you have a porn problem—a majority of the world has a porn problem. You shouldn't be ashamed to pull aside someone you trust and tell them, "Hey, man, I'm trying to do things right with God. The problem is I have a porn issue. I'm committed to stopping, but I want to make sure I never go back. So, I'm putting your name on this app. That way if I ever screw up, you're going to know." If you do that, there's a much greater chance you're not going to fail, because you don't want that dude's cell phone ringing. Ready to do it—right here, right now? Google "porn accountability app," choose your best option, then unplug that Wi-Fi!

Get rid of the opportunities and get accountability—both are so important. The first for the short term and the second for the long term. When you're first looking to break the habit, you need to do all you can to limit the possibilities of failing. That's why you cancel the Wi-Fi. But after a while when you've built up your resistance, you may feel it's time to let the internet back into your life. That's when the accountability becomes so important, because you never know when some porn is going to pop up on the screen.

In Galatians 5, we're told that we have a choice about who we're going to follow. We've got one of two options—the sinful nature or the Spirit. "The sinful nature wants to do evil, which is just the opposite of what the Spirit wants. And the Spirit gives us desires that are the opposite of what the sinful nature desires" (v. 17). There's no middle ground—you're going to follow one or the other. You choose darkness—the sinful nature—or light. What happens when you choose the darkness? "Now the works of the flesh are evident: sexual immorality, impurity, sensuality, idolatry, sorcery, enmity, strife, jealousy, fits of anger, rivalries, dissensions, divisions, envy, drunkenness, orgies, and things like these. I warn you, as I warned you before, that those who do such things will not inherit the kingdom of God" (vv. 19–21 ESV). When you're going after Satan's shiny objects—living the sinful life—these things will just come naturally. It's not like you're going to have to wake up one morning and decide, "You know, I think I'll indulge a few body appetites today." Fulfilling your body appetites becomes your jam.

But if you decide instead that you are not going to take the bait—instead of following the flesh, you're going to follow the Spirit, the Light—the results are very different. "But the Holy Spirit produces this kind of fruit in our lives: love, joy, peace, patience, kindness, goodness, faithfulness, gentleness, and self-control" (Galatians 5:22–23). We talked about this spiritual fruit in the last chapter. You don't have to work at producing spiritual apples; they just come naturally. Let me tell you, as someone who has produced both kinds of fruit—cranking out those beautiful, delicious, crunchy spiritual apples is so much better than pushing out the nasty, soft, brown, rotted, worm-filled fruit that comes from following Satan and my own desires. The spiritual fruit not only makes my life so much better physically and spiritually, but it also betters the lives of everyone around me.

Again, it all comes back to that decision to tell God, "Not my will, but Yours be done." It's a simple prayer, but it's game-changing and your life will never be the same. When you pray that prayer, Satan's going to attack. Don't fight the battle alone. Take an accountability buddy along for the fight. Keep no secrets. You get his back and let him get yours. Together you'll take down the enemy.

FOCUS ON CONVICTION, NOT CONDEMNATION

The devil wants you to know that you suck as a Christian—he's really good at that. So, he's going to tell you every chance he gets. Every time you screw up and give in to your body appetites, he's going to be right there saying, "See! You can't do the Christian life. It's no use. You're a total hypocrite and a big poser. You aren't fooling anybody. God's given up on you by now. You might as well give up, too."

But you want to know something? Jesus also knows that you suck as a Christian—and He still loves you. That doesn't mean that He doesn't care when we do the wrong things. Sin is still bad. It still hurts us, hurts others, and hurts our relationship with God. But God also knows that we're going to mess up and that we are a work in progress. And knowing that we're going to mess up, He's already provided a way for us to take care of that sin like we talked about in an earlier chapter—"If we confess our sins to him, he is faithful and just to forgive us our sins and to cleanse us from all wickedness" (1 John 1:9). The blood that Jesus shed on the cross washes us white as snow. We get cleansed by torrents of living water and we're empowered by the Holy Spirit.

The devil and the Holy Spirit couldn't be more different in the way they deal with us. Satan is there to condemn us—to tell us how miserable we are. If you ever have the thought that God hates you or is done with you—if you ever think that you are so far gone that Jesus will never forgive you—that thought is not from God. It's a lie and it's right from the mouth of the devil.

The Bible tells us something very different: "So now there is no condemnation for those who belong to Christ Jesus" (Romans 8:1). Once we have given our hearts to God, He will never turn His back on us, ever! He loves us, and He always will. King David was thinking one day about how much God loved him, and he wrote, "How precious are your thoughts about me, O God. They cannot be numbered! I can't even count them; they outnumber the grains of sand! And when I wake up, you are still with me!" (Psalm 139:17–18). Don't buy into the devil's lie—God never thinks of you with anything except love in His heart.

Instead of condemning us *for* our sin, God convicts us *of* our sin. Instead of saying, "You sinned; now you have to pay," Jesus says, "You sinned, but I've already paid." Instead of saying, "Your sin has permanently separated you from God," the Holy Spirit says, "Let's deal with this sin so that you can be made right again with God." One is hopeless; the other is full of hope. One leads to death; the other leads to an incredible, forgiven life.

You have to understand that everybody sins. "If we claim we have no sin, we are only fooling ourselves and not living in the truth" (1 John 1:8). None of us is perfect. We are all just sinners saved by grace. We don't use that as an excuse to keep on sinning. If we don't have a desire to stop the sin, then we have to really think about whether we are actually Christians. But we also have to make sure that we don't let sin cause us to doubt our salvation or God's love.

Think about a baby growing up. First, he learns to crawl, then walk, then run. When he's first learning to walk, there are a lot of stumbles and falls. Can you imagine a dad getting mad at his kid every time he tripped over his feet or fell on his butt?

What kind of a father would punish their kid for that? What dad would say, "You stupid kid! Why don't you walk already?" Why would we think that God is like that? He understands that we are going to fall as we learn to walk the Christian life. When you find yourself on your butt, get up and start walking again. Don't buy into the devil's lie that God's done with you. He's not, and you can count on that. Keep moving forward— walking gets a lot easier the more steps you take.

GET READY TO FIGHT

Living for Christ is a battle. Like I said, it was a six-month struggle before I finally had the strength to say no to porn. But that was just to stop watching it. The fight to resist it went on for years and still hits me at times. Even today I still have urges and thoughts of porn. Just a few days ago in church I had all these crazy thoughts of sex and stuff flashing through my mind. The Bible talks about the "fiery arrows of the devil" that he shoots at us (Ephesians 6:16). I literally had to close my eyes because I didn't want to look at any of the girls leading worship. How sick is that? But that's just the devil casting out his shiny lures. If I hadn't prepared myself ahead of time, I easily could have bit at his hook and he would have taken my mind for a ride in fantasyland.

Paul talked about how he trained himself to fight the spiritual battle. He said, "I run with purpose in every step. I am not just shadowboxing. I discipline my body like an athlete, training it to do what it should. Otherwise, I fear that after preaching to others I myself might be disqualified" (1 Corinthians 9:26–27). He didn't want to leave church one day after preaching a sermon about purity only to get caught an hour later down the street dancing the forbidden dance with the harp player from the worship team. He knew the fight was real, and he was in constant training.

I've taken Paul's example to heart. I work hard each day to make sure I'm healthy physically and spiritually. Here's a typical day for me: I wake up in the morning. First thing I do is get coffee—of course. Then I go upstairs and turn on the KWAVE radio app, which is a Bible-teaching radio station. I start my workout doing stretches and working with weights. I usually get about an hour in, which means in those sixty minutes I've worked out both my body and my spirit. From there, I'll pull out my Bible and read a chapter of Proverbs. Thirty-one chapters in Proverbs, thirty-one days in a month—I just read whatever chapter matches the date. Then I read my devotion for the day.

After that I go to the skate park. Thirty-minute drive there and I'm listening to a Bible study that is going from Genesis to Revelation. I just pick up wherever I left off. If I'm not feeling the Bible study, then I'll hit the Bible app and get some audio-Bible time in. I get to the park and I start skating— more physical training. I skate for an hour; then I head back home. That's another thirty minutes for the Bible study or for listening to whatever else I'm in the mood for. It's all about time management and self-discipline. That's my morning. In that three-hour time frame, I've trained both my body and my spirit for the day ahead. Now I'm ready to launch into work— whatever God has planned for me to get done.

You may not have that much time in the morning, but you do have some. Even if it means getting up earlier, find a way to make it work. The only people who don't have time to physically and spiritually train are those who don't want to physically and spiritually train. It may mean cutting out an hour of TV or video games. If you want to get real, then look at the screen time amount on your phone. All that time on social media and playing games is time that you're never going to get back. We all have time if we're not wasting time. Fitting in a daily appointment with God may cost you an hour of sleep, but He will pay you that hour back. He'll give you extra energy and strength. He'll keep you focused and help you to get more done than you normally would. God knows your schedule—trust Him; He'll make it work. God can get more done in five minutes than you can get done in your whole life.

———

Get rid of the sin opportunities, get some accountability in your life, focus on the Holy Spirit's conviction, not the devil's condemnation, and train yourself for the fight. All these will help you to keep tight with the Spirit. The Bible says, "Since we are living by the Spirit, let us follow the Spirit's leading in every part of our lives" (Galatians 5:25). The words "let us follow the Spirit's leading" literally mean "let us walk with the Spirit" or "let us keep in step with the Spirit." Have you ever seen soldiers marching in ranks, everyone lined up and keeping in step with the drill sergeant? That's how we're to be with the Holy Spirit. When we are in step with Him, we'll be able to recognize when

He's talking with us. We'll be able to hear when He puts up the stop signs in our lives. What are stop signs?

Let's say I'm coming home from work and I'm getting those crazy thoughts that end up turning into urges to check out some pornography. There's going to be a prompting in my mind—a stop sign, a thought—that says, "Yeah, I shouldn't be doing this. Why? Because I'm a Christian. I'm not doing this stuff anymore." But then I put that stop sign out of my mind and I continue driving. When I get home, I start making my way up to my room knowing darn well what I'm going to do. I open the door and see my laptop—BOOM: another stop sign. "Dude, do not open that computer!" I push that stop sign out of the way, grab my laptop, and flip it open. I turn it on—BOOM: "Seriously, dude, do not go to Google!" I ignore the stop sign and I start typing in the Google search—BOOM: "Don't click Play!" Another prompting—another stop sign.

Those stop signs—that's the work of the Holy Spirit. It's His voice inside of you. And He's not speaking Old English with a bunch of "thees" and "thous" and "thines." You may say, "Well, I don't hear God's voice—never mind if He's speaking like Shakespeare or not." Yes, you do. When you feel those promptings, that's God telling you, "Don't do it!" For God to speak, you don't have to actually hear a booming voice coming down from heaven saying, "Stop watching porn!" It's not a lack of Him talking; it's a lack of us listening.

If you want to live right for God, you can. If you want to be able to see the shiny objects before you feel the hook in your mouth, just listen. Know this—the devil is not interested in catch-and-release fishing. He wants to reel you in and kill you.

He wants to see you thrown in hell. But when you train yourself in the Bible and you connect with the Holy Spirit through prayer, God will give you everything you need to recognize those shiny objects for what they are. He will give you the strength and self-control so you can live a life that makes both you and Him incredibly proud.

CHAPTER 7

Destroy All Gods

Some people ask me, "Ryan, what happened to you? Wasn't your dad like this well-known pastor with a huge church? How'd you go so far off the rails?" It's a good question, and I don't know that I have the answer. I just know that sometimes it happens. Maybe someday someone will do a big research project and interview a thousand pastors' kids who went off the path. All I know is that there are times when things happen to the children of church leaders and that, sadly, I'm not the only one. In fact, I know many who followed the same road I did.

The same things that happen to pastors' kids today sometimes happened to the kids of kings back in the Old Testament days. One prime example was Manasseh, the son of King Hezekiah. The Bible says, "Hezekiah trusted in the LORD, the

God of Israel. There was no one like him among all the kings of Judah, either before or after his time. He remained faithful to the LORD in everything, and he carefully obeyed all the commands the LORD had given Moses" (2 Kings 18:5–6). Hezekiah had grown the kingdom, he had military victories, and people loved him. One time when he was told he was going to die, he cried out to God and God gave him another fifteen years to live. Hezekiah totally had God's favor.

When Hezekiah died, his son Manasseh took over. There was one thing Manasseh knew going in, and that was that he was never going to be like Dad. He wasn't down with that program—not in a million years, not even close. He grew up in his dad's shadow, so he knew, "People are going to compare me to my father, then tell me how great he was." He didn't want to be some knockoff version of his dad—he wanted to do things his way, live his lifestyle, be his own person. And that's what he did.

Manasseh wasn't playing games when he took over—the dude went nuts. Everything his dad did, he went in the opposite direction. Every kind of sin there was to commit, he did it three times. It's like sin was a salad bar and it was all you can eat. Partying, marrying a ton of women, keeping a bunch more around just for hookups. I totally get that sex-addicted life— I used to call girls at 2:00 a.m. for booty calls after the bars closed. When it came to following God, Manasseh didn't want anything to do with Him. This king actually went into the Temple—basically, their main church—and he had them worshipping the stars, meaning the zodiac of those days, right in the holy areas. He was into witchcraft and magic, necromancy and mediums. "Medium" is just another word for "psychic," where demons speak through people. Manasseh was into all sorts of gnarly stuff. He made idols and put them up everywhere for the people to worship. Just think how crazy it was to have all this kind of stuff in the actual church of that day. Imagine walking into a church today and instead of having a Bible study, they're holding a séance. You would trip!

One idol he spread around was that of the goddess Ashtoreth. They'd make these statues of her in all these pornographic positions in order to arouse the sexual appetites. It was basically just porn packaged differently. The people would come in to worship, see the porn statues, get all aroused, and they'd break out into orgies. This was how they worshipped Ashtoreth. It would get totally out of control and they'd be doing all kinds of crazy NSFW stuff. It was basically XXX porn without the cameras. Like King Solomon said, "History merely repeats itself. It has all been done before. Nothing under the sun is truly new" (Ecclesiastes 1:9).

What happens after you sleep with all these random people worshipping their gods? You get babies. But the girls that were in the "worship" ceremonies would be like, "Yo, I'm eighteen and I don't even know whose baby this is." So now you have unwanted babies. It's just like today. You watch porn—all kinds of crazy stuff online. Your sex drive comes alive. You're single and maybe you're even trying to walk the right path with God. But you're into this porn, you get aroused, and you end up sleeping with some random person to fulfill your fantasy. And then suddenly she's pregnant, and you're like, "I don't even know this girl. This was supposed to be just some one-night stand. We've got to get rid of this baby." So, what do you do?

If you were living back then, you'd take the easy way out. You'd say, "Let's worship the pleasure god Molech. Let's get the fires burning in that golden calf god." Once the metal would get white-hot, they'd pass the baby through the fire and into the searing hands of Molech. In other words, they'd toss the baby into the flames. The problem is the babies would start screaming from the pain. Well, no one wanted to hear that, so they started beating on drums. That's where the tradition of drum circles began. You slam the mallets on the drumheads hard enough, you can't hear the babies crying as they burned to death. Talk about disgusting.

What happens today? Again, you watch the porn, you get aroused, you sleep with some girl. She gets pregnant. You say, "I'm too young. I've got to live my life. This baby is just going to be in the way. I don't want this thing. Let's go abort it." So you go to the abortion clinic and they inject your baby with liquid fire. The innocent child dies a horribly painful death, but at least it's not going to inconvenience you or interfere with your plans for your life. Molech or abortion clinic. It's the same thing, just packaged differently.

———

That's the kind of crazy stuff that happens when we put any gods before the true God. What are these little "g" gods? Think of it this way—Jesus said to love the Lord your God with all your heart, soul, mind, and strength. Who is that Lord? It's Jesus Himself. That's why we call Him our Lord and Savior. When we call Him Lord Jesus, "Lord" is not His name. It's a title. The word literally means "master." So, when I say that Jesus Christ is my Lord, that means with everything I've got I'm going to do what He says to do and not do what He says not to do. God is against going out and sleeping around. He's against porn. He's against drugs and greed and anger and all these kinds of things that destroy your life anyway. If I'm doing the things that God is against, then that means that I'm putting something else ahead of Him. He isn't my God anymore. He's been taken off the throne in my life for something else I love more.

We've got to destroy all gods—any of those little idols that take the place of the real God in our lives. Think about your life—what is your god? Is it your job? Is it money? I remember seeing this famous preacher begging for money. He said, "Send me your cash and I'll send you some anointing oil." I heard about another pastor who said he needed a $65 million Learjet in order to spread the Gospel of Jesus Christ. That's false. That's corrupt. That's them chasing their gods.

For some it's relationships, sports, or careers. For others it's porn or alcohol or weed. Some are into witchcraft and the Ouija board. More and more people these days are worshipping pills. So many are taking these prescription drugs not because they need them, but because they're hooked on them. I know a lot who are in rehab because of this stuff. They got a surgery, took the pills for their pain, now they can't shake them. I'm not saying you should never take a pain pill if the doc prescribes it after a surgery or a medical problem. Do what you have to do, but then get off it as fast as you can.

It's very unlikely that you have an idol of Molech or Ashtoreth in your house. People would probably look at you all weird if you did. If you are putting anything before the one true God, then you are worshipping it. You don't need some shiny statue of a god that you bow down to—idols today are packaged differently. Satan's gotten a bit smarter in these last days.

How do we destroy all these gods? We repent. We make a U-turn from the stuff that we're doing. We make Jesus our Master and receive the power of the Holy Spirit. Jesus said, "You will receive power when the Holy Spirit comes upon you" (Acts 1:8). That is the only way. Most of these gods we've talked about were mine at some time. It was through the power of the Holy Spirit that God took away my drug and alcohol problems overnight. Then, over time He took the porn and the cigarettes and the f-bombs. One day I was like, "Hey, has anyone heard me say the f-word lately?" Everyone said, "No! That's crazy!" I'm like, "Right on!" All things pass away and are made new. That's what Jesus does. He's in the business of killing gods and transforming lives. That's who He's always been and that's who He'll always be. He's the same yesterday, today, and forever—He'll never change.

Not too long after Jesus started His public ministry, He chose His disciples. There were a bunch of guys hanging around Him, following Him wherever He went. But He decided that He was going to choose twelve to be His squad—His inner circle that He was going to teach and mentor with hands-on ministry training. When you look at these guys, it's easy to find yourself wondering what Jesus was thinking. This was a straight-up motley crew.

Look at these guys! First, you have James and John, known as the Sons of Thunder. Why? These guys seemed to have some anger problems. I can totally relate. Once, when Jesus and the disciples were going to pass through Samaria, the

Samaritans—who hated Jews—said, "Uh, you ain't coming through here with a crew. No way." The Sons of Thunder took their shot: "Hey, Jesus, let's call fire down from heaven! Smoke these fools; burn them up!" That's how the Sons of Thunder were—loose cannons for sure. Today they'd probably be called The Nuclear Boys.

Then you have Matthew the tax collector. Remember, we talked about him a few chapters back. Everybody hated him because tax collectors were all crooks. Then there was the radical political zealot, the paranoid doubter, and all those blue-collar fishermen. And of course, Judas the scumbag—the biggest poser in the Bible. He was the one who betrayed Jesus. Judas was a liar and was stealing money from their money bag—chasing after his little god of greed. These were Jesus' disciples, the ones He chose. They were just common people. They're just like you and me. But Jesus took these everyday people and did some amazing things. He said, "Follow Me," and they followed Him. These were the dudes that changed the world, and we're still talking about them today—learning from their successes and failures.

One day Jesus said, "Okay, guys, we're going to the city. We're going to check out Jerusalem and see what's crackin'." It was a few days' travel to get where they were going—walking down the dusty roads in sandals and sleeping under trees. They didn't have any $65 million jets to fly them down, paid by church tithes. They weren't staying in thousand-dollar-a-night hotels or ballin' in the presidential suite at the W Hotel, acting like they're celebrities. So, when they finally made it to the city and went walking through the gates, they were probably looking like straight-up savages compared to all the city slickers.

They got to the Temple, and the disciples could probably see that something was going on with Jesus. He was getting all agitated like He was about to set it off. From the outside, everything at the Temple looked good. There were something like 2.5 million people crammed together in Jerusalem for the once-a-year Passover feast. Talk about a major BBQ! In the huge altar, the fires were burning and the sacrifices were cooking off on top. It all looked like a well-oiled priestly worship machine. But Jesus could see behind the curtain. It was like the Wizard of Oz. Everyone was amazed at the power of the wizard, but then they pulled back the curtain and there's some dude back there pushing buttons and pulling levers. It was all a huge fraud. Jesus looked past the curtain of the Temple and saw that it was all corrupt—a huge religious scam.

When the people came to the feast, they were supposed to bring animals for the sacrifice. But some came from a long way away. Others lived in cities, so they weren't raising animals. So the priests said, "Hey, if you want to make a sacrifice, it's no use bringing your own animal or buying one from so far away. Just purchase one from us." But when the people showed up, they'd charge them double the price. This made it hard for the common folk—the blue collars and the poor—to worship God. And there was no place else they could go, because the priests made sure that they were the only place in town that people could buy the animals.

So, the visitors were forced to ante up their Roman coins to the animal vendors. But then the priests would say, "No, we can't accept those nasty, sinful Roman coins. You've got to go exchange them for the Temple shekel—God's holy cash." Of course, the only place they could do that was at the tables of the

Temple money changers, who would tax the exchange at 25 percent. So, by the time they were done, they'd just bought some
sketchy-looking sheep for double the price with Temple shekels
that they'd paid a 25 percent premium on. God's people were
getting ripped off by God's leaders, who didn't care at all about
the people. All they cared about was making money.

So, what would Jesus do? Simple answer—He'd kick some
butt. The Bible says that Jesus made a whip out of rope, then
went after the religious leaders. He chased every one of them
out of the Temple, cracking His whip to make sure they moved
fast. Just picture it. The Temple was huge, and Jesus was running around everywhere, chasing people out from behind pillars
and through doorways. The Bible says He chased them all out—
every last one of them. The disciples were probably tripping hard
at this point. "He just asked us to follow Him, and now here
we are?"

But Jesus wasn't done after he cleared the people out. He
came back and started chasing out all the animals. Most of the
disciples were watching and wondering, "Dude, what is happening here? The Roman guards got their eyes on us, probably
ready to serve us a beatdown and take us off to jail." Instead,
the Romans guards were probably sitting there dying laughing,
saying, "It's about time these guys got what they deserved." I
know I would. Peter was probably feeding off the energy, hoping
to get in the game—"Any of these fools rolls up on me and I'm
knocking him out." The Sons of Thunder would have been saying, "How about now, Jesus? Now's the time to call down that
fire from heaven. Light it up and burn it down!"

Once the animals were gone, Jesus still wasn't done. He
came back again and knocked over all the money changers'

tables—pouring out all their boxes onto the ground. He was probably kicking the coins all around, saying, "Get this dirty money out of My Father's house." The Bible says He was moved with compassion for the people. He was on fire for God's house. He was fulfilling the Old Testament prophecy that said, "Passion for your house has consumed me" (Psalm 69:9). He was flipping over tables—chucking chairs across the Temple and destroying the marketplace. That's Jesus with His righteous anger. In Him you see the difference between anger used the way it should be and an anger problem. Jesus was standing for what was right, and that's what righteous anger is.

Another way to tell that it was righteous anger and not just Jesus blowing a gasket is that when Jesus had made His point, He stopped. He probably got all the disciples together and explained from the Scriptures why He had to do what He did. Then His passion for God turned into compassion for the people. Remember, there were about 2.5 million people in the city at that time. Can you imagine how many miracles Jesus did? He had shown everyone in the Temple that the religious leaders had made money and power their gods. And then in one righteous action, He had shown how weak their gods were.

Sometimes God has to flip the tables in our lives, too. That's what happened to me in that hotel room in Panama City. I had made pleasure, sex, drugs, and the party scene my gods. Jesus came and destroyed the temple I had built for these false gods, showing me how empty that kind of life was. It hurt—it woke me up. But it was the best thing that ever happened to me. If your life is in pieces around you right now, maybe it's Jesus destroying your gods—showing you that what you've made number one in your life, your master passion, doesn't deserve to be in that place. If you clean house in every room of your life and get rid of all that junk, putting God in His proper place, you'll be amazed at the changes you see take place one day at a time.

A little while later, Jesus and His disciples relocated down by the Jordan River and began baptizing people. By the way, "disciple" is just another word for a die-hard student. Imagine having a teacher that you're so amped about that you're willing to follow them around wherever they go just so you can learn more and more from them. This kind of relationship where a teacher intentionally built into the life of a student 24/7 was pretty common back in Jesus' day. This is similar to what I do when I take young people on The Whosoevers tours, so they can watch what happens and learn how to reach out to others. The best learning doesn't always take place in classrooms.

John the Baptist had his own little group of disciples. They were down at another part of the river doing their own baptism thing with all the people who were coming their way. When they'd come to John the Baptist, he'd preach to them a message of repentance. Remember, to repent means to stop doing the sin you're doing and start doing the opposite. You confess your sins, you commit to not doing it anymore, and God will forgive you and continue to change your life. What's happened in different places in our culture is that the word "repent" has gotten a bad rap. I've seen guys outside of concerts with their signs that say, REPENT! GOD HATES GAYS! and other things like that. They've even told me that I wasn't a Christian. Those guys are kooks, okay? What they're saying is not true. God loves sinners. He loves alcoholics and drug addicts. He loves liars and murderers. And, guess what. He loves the LGBT community, too. He also loves that judgmental Christian who thinks he has it all figured out. God loves everyone—you and me. He came to forgive all of us of the things we do wrong—yes, all of our sins, every one of those times we give in to our body appetites. God may not like what you're doing, but He still loves you to death—yes, all the way to death on the cross.

That's the message that John the Baptist was telling these people. "Hey, if you're out there lying, stop lying and turn to God. If you're sleeping with some guy's wife, stop sleeping with that guy's wife and turn to God. If you're being greedy, stop being greedy. If you're using drugs, stop using drugs." Basically, he's telling them that if you're being a bad boy or a bad girl, stop! You need to turn from your sins—the little gods you've put on the thrones in your lives—and turn to the real God. Again, that's repentance. Jesus loves you, and He'll help you change your life—no problem is too big. How amazing is that message for a dirty sinner like me? Sign me up with that grace and mercy and forgiveness all day long. Plus, He will transform my life and I get to go to heaven, too? Sign! Me! Up!

What I love about John is that he stuck to his calling. Even though Jesus' ministry had started up and people were starting to go to Him instead of John, he kept doing what God was telling him to do. Sometimes people get all weird about that kind of stuff—like there's some kind of competition in the church.

Imagine if God was leading you to start passing out sandwiches to hungry people downtown. You get it going and you're feeding a hundred people every time you go out. But then suddenly your numbers drop and you're only feeding seventy-five. You check out what's going on and discover that somebody else has started passing out sandwiches two blocks away. How are you going to react? Are you going to get all bummed out because someone is stealing hungry people from you? Or are you going to say, "Thank you, Jesus, for multiplying Your workers! There are plenty of hungry people to go around!" The more people there are going about the Father's business, the better.

Competition makes no sense when it comes to the things of God. All these voices around us tell us that we have to be the best or have the biggest or be the most important. Those voices aren't from God. That's why we have to kill that noise; otherwise, we'll fall into the trap of wanting what other people have. Remember, God is the One who promotes and demotes. He's the One who calls the shots.

So John kept doing what he was called to do, and people kept coming to him—maybe not as many as before, but enough. And God blessed him. But then along comes this dude looking to start a division. "A debate broke out between John's disciples and a certain Jew over ceremonial cleansing" (John 3:25). This is so typical. God is doing great work, and then some religious guy comes along to divide people. I'll be somewhere and a bunch of people are getting saved, and some religious guy will come up and say, "Hey, I like everything you were doing, but punk rock Jesus?" Because he likes to picture Jesus holding a sweet little lamb in a green pasture like the pictures from second-grade Sunday school. My friend Sonny from P.O.D. calls those guys the "but" men. God works, people get saved, but…The "but" men are pure comedy.

These guys feel it's their job to always find something wrong. They believe that God has blessed them with the spiritual gift of criticism. But it's really that they're caught up in dead religion. They're all about traditions and not about God. This guy who was arguing with John's disciples is a perfect example. In the midst of John the Baptist's amazing ministry with people getting saved and turning to God, this guy started giving them a hard time because they weren't following the Jewish traditions of washing their hands in just the right way.

This hand washing wasn't even in the Bible. The Jews from before that time had decided that the Bible needed a little extra content, so they came up with their own rules—thousands of them compiled over the centuries. These man-made additions to God's Word were designed to help explain what they believed God really meant by what He had said in the Bible. But it was totally unnecessary. If God said, "Thou shalt not kill," then don't kill. If God said, "Thou shalt not lie," then don't lie. If Jesus says that you will receive power when the Holy Spirit comes upon you, then you will receive power. I don't need a translator for that. But these guys decided to put in their additions and explanations; then they started following those additions—their man-made traditions—more than the Bible itself.

Don't believe that this just happened back then. You still find these man-made additions all through the church today. When electric guitars first came out, a lot of people thought they were instruments of the devil. They believed that if you brought an electric guitar into church and played it for worship, then you were going to hell. That was totally a man-made judgment call.

Have you ever read in the Bible where God condemns electric guitars? If so, then show me. "Thou shalt not play the guitar of electricity, lest thou endest up on the highway to hell." Please. God loves it when we go all out in worship of Him. If King David's harp had an input jack, you know he would have been jamming to all those psalms. Let's not get caught up in traditions. Instead, let's get caught up in that Spirit-led life and the Scripture—following His lead and doing the things He wants us to do.

Somehow in the midst of this debate about hand washing, Jesus' name came up. Who knows? Maybe the religious guy took a jab at them, saying how everyone was all excited about Jesus and how John the Baptist was quickly becoming a has-been. So John's disciples interrupted his baptizing and said, "Rabbi, the man you met on the other side of the Jordan River, the one you identified as the Messiah, is also baptizing people. And everybody is going to him instead of coming to us" (John 3:26). So, John's disciples were bringing him up to speed. "Hey, man, you know that One you said is the Son of God? Dude, it's going down. All the people are going to Him to get baptized."

They thought that John was going to be all upset about this, but they got the exact opposite response. "No one can receive anything unless God gives it from heaven. You yourselves know how plainly I told you, 'I am not the Messiah. I am only here to prepare the way for him'" (John 3:27–28). Understand, John was a man that God had used big-time. God hadn't spoken to His people for over four hundred years; then suddenly John the Baptist gets called to start talking for Him. Not only that, but the message he's bringing is that the Messiah is coming. This was a gnarly position. But what was John's attitude? He didn't at all get caught up in the glory.

You know how people can seem to want the glory for themselves that really belongs to God? "Yeah, dude, I spoke and did you see how many people got saved? I'm pretty dope. I don't know if you know this, but I'm kind of a big deal." Stupid! That's not you. That's God. That's the Holy Spirit working in you and through you. If anyone gets saved from reading this book, it's not me. I'm just here to talk about Jesus. The Holy Spirit is the One who convicts the world of sin. That's what He does. I'm nobody. I'm just a guy who sucks at reading and math and anything else that has to do with school. Don't get tripped up in your head. John was saying to his disciples, "I'm not the Messiah, you guys. Why are you all freaking out? What's going on over there is amazing."

John went on to tell them, "It is the bridegroom who marries the bride, and the bridegroom's friend is simply glad to stand with him and hear his vows. Therefore, I am filled with joy at his success" (John 3:29). When you go to a wedding, nobody cares about the best man. No one's saying, "I'm so happy for Ryan. He gets to dress in a tux and stand next to the dude getting married." The groom is the big deal. John the Baptist is saying, "I'm just stoked to be in the wedding." Jesus Christ was coming, and John was thrilled to help prepare the way.

If you're telling people about Jesus, then you are being John the Baptist. If you're telling them what Christ has done for them and how they can find forgiveness and peace and salvation in Him through repentance, then you are preparing the way for Jesus to come into their hearts. There's only one Bridegroom, but it's a blessing just to be in the wedding.

John then made a beautiful statement that tells us exactly who he is. He said, "He must become greater and greater, and I must become less and less" (John 3:30). Exactly! Life goals! John just nailed it! This is the little-god-destroying commitment that will keep us right with Jesus. Let God increase, while I decrease. How can God increase in our lives? We need to confess our sins daily. We pray, "Lord, show me what I need to confess. Show me the secret things in my life that You don't like." Confess those things and receive forgiveness. Then read your Bible. The more you read the Bible, the more Jesus Christ will manifest in you and transform your life. Pray—every day, throughout the day. They could be long prayers or just little quick ones to keep you connected to the Holy Spirit. Get around other Christians. You have the same minds, the same Lord, the same Savior. You can feed off each other and hold one another accountable.

Finally, you need to ask the Holy Spirit to show you the little gods you have in your life. What do you have that is taking the place of God? What is decreasing His presence in you? Maybe you're saying, "I'm a Christian, but I'm not feeling His presence right now." What are your gods? Do the inventory.

This brings us back to Jesus' command to us to pick up our cross and follow Him. We do that by destroying all those things that we're putting ahead of Him. Destroy all those gods. Deny self. Sacrifice yourself for the Lord and for others. Grab those things that are taking you away from God—that are causing you to decrease God—take them to the cross and kill them. The cross is a beautiful place, but it's also a place of murder, bloodshed, and pain. It's not going to be easy to not watch pornographic things, to not sleep with your girlfriend, to not go out and drink. In fact, you won't be able to do it on your own.

The only way you can destroy those gods is with the power of the Holy Spirit in your life.

John finished his conversation with his disciples by saying, "The Father loves his Son and has put everything into his hands. And anyone who believes in God's Son has eternal life. Anyone who doesn't obey the Son will never experience eternal life but remains under God's angry judgment" (John 3:35–36). What does John say you need to do to get eternal life? Absolutely nothing. Salvation isn't about doing—it's about believing. He didn't talk about going to church. Church is good—it's where you can learn about Jesus. But salvation has nothing to do with religion. All you have to do is believe that Jesus Christ died on the cross for your sins. Believe that He rose again on the third day. And when you believe that, ask God to come into your life. When you do, He will send the Holy Spirit into your life. And then you will be one with Christ, because the Father, the Son, and the Holy Spirit are all one.

Now that He's in your life, He will lead you and guide you. He will light up your life. My friend Nick told me that after he gave his life to God, he started hearing the birds chirping. You'll be shocked at how beautiful and green everything is. The Holy Spirit enriches our lives and makes everything so much better. The dopest thing about it all is that you can talk to God and He'll talk back. He has a plan for your life. He says He's going to be a light for your feet so that you'll know where to go (see Psalm 119:105). If ever your life gets crooked and feels like it's spinning out of control, He says that He's going to come and make your crooked path straight.

We are all created with a purpose. The problem is that we let these little gods come into our lives and get us off course. They are the distracting white noise that keeps us from hearing the voice of God. When we destroy those gods, God will give us a life like we've never dreamed of. But you're never going to find out what that life is like or what He has planned for you until you get rid of the false gods and give your life to the real One. You can do that—right here, right now. Put the book down, close your eyes, and ask Jesus to come into your life. He's there waiting, and He'll change everything.

CHAPTER 8

God's Signs in the Storms

The dark clouds start rolling in. Lightning flashes like a strobe light. A fraction of a second later comes a massive clap of thunder—the boom followed by its echo crackling all around you. The rain begins, coming down lightly at first. But then it increases and soon it's pouring. In a matter of seconds, you're soaked from head to toe. You're not a fool, so you run for cover. Why? Because nobody wants to get caught out in the storm.

A storm is a disrupter to everything in its path. It destroys music festivals. It shuts down sporting events and skate park sessions. It ruins birthday parties and wedding receptions, making everybody duck for cover. Depending on its intensity, a storm can bring floods, uproot trees, snap power lines, spread disease, mess up water systems, and pollute the ocean from its runoff.

Unless you are already safe inside, there is little chance that you will be able to continue whatever activity you were engaged in when the storm first hit. Storms bring change and difficulties.

But contrary to popular opinion, not all storms come to disrupt our life; some come to clear our path. Read that sentence again. When hard times—storms—hit us, we automatically assume the worst-case scenario. "This is going to be terrible." "How am I going to survive this?" "I'm tired; I can't go through this again." "God must really hate me." And those statements may all be at least partly true—not the "God hates me" part, but the fact that the storm very well might be terrible. There could be pain, there could be grief; you could end up injured, you could end up broke. Storms suck, especially when you're in the middle of one.

The thing is there is meaning above the madness of the storms. Sometimes God allows the crazy times to come because He's getting ready to do something new and amazing in our lives. He may be using the hard time to clear some junk and get us to a place where we're ready to grow. He might be moving us out of our comfort zones so that He can put us in amazing new places. Sometimes He gives us stormy seasons to build our faith. As I'm writing this chapter, I'm on day thirty-five of Orange County, California, being on lockdown because of COVID-19. There is unrest and fear all around me. I had to put half my Whosoevers team on furlough, and thank God He was able to get them full-time jobs at Costco.

But still some days I battle with anxiety and stress. Today is a perfect example as I have to decide on more budget cuts. This is a major storm, and I don't know what the outcome will be. However, I know that God is on His throne. It's in these moments that I have to remind myself of God's promises that He has given to us in the Bible. I tell God, "The Whosoevers is Your movement. That means making this budget work is Your problem, not mine." That's when I find peace even though there is all this noise and madness around me. I don't know for sure if The Whosoevers will still be in business thirty days from now or if I'll have enough food for my family. But whatever path God leads us down, we know that we can walk it through faith, obedience, and trust.

It all comes down to perspective. If you're only looking at what is immediately in front of you, then every second of the storm is going to be exhausting. But if your vision is further forward to what can be and you are putting your faith in the Word of God, then you will be able to lift your focus above the pain and confusion so you can feel the joy of God's plan even in the worst of times. The Bible says, "And we know that God causes everything to work together for the good of those who love God and are called according to his purpose for them" (Romans 8:28). Even when it looks like everything is falling apart, God is actually putting the pieces together. We may not see it, but that's when faith comes in.

It was right when I met the girl of my dreams that the crap hit the fan in my life. Other than meeting Jesus Christ, finding this girl was the best thing that had ever happened to me. She's the one that I had been waiting for, searching for, praying for. Life was really great—and then it wasn't. It was like a split-second shift. The bottom dropped out, my world turned upside down, and God started moving and shaking and transforming my life.

Rewind a few months from the fan hitting, and let's pick up the story there. The Whosoevers Movement was in a great place. It had been about four years since that first meeting between Lacey, Head, Sonny, and me, and God had been blowing the ministry up ever since. Doors were opening everywhere and I was speaking all the time—sharing my story and spreading the Gospel. Thousands of people were getting saved, some were getting healed—we even cast a few demons out of people. The Holy Spirit was moving powerfully everywhere we went.

Much of my time was spent touring with bands, hitting up music festivals with Sonny and Head. A sample week would see me on tour in Australia with Korn. I'd attend the music festival with Head and Fieldy (Korn's bassist) on the weekend, spending my time talking to the other bands on the tour, developing relationships, and loving people. Then I'd go out on my own Monday through Friday, doing three to four Whosoevers speaking engagements a day in churches and conferences and schools and rehabs. Any place that would open their door—whether it was for five people or thousands—I'd go there and talk about Christ. When the weekend came around again, I'd fly to the next city to connect back up with the band for the next concert. Basically, I was just trying to follow Jesus' example in the Gospels by going from town to town, city to city, loving on all the people who God put in my path.

During this time, I was also producing concerts. There was one large music festival outreach that I produced each year that would have between twelve thousand and eighteen thousand attending, depending on the city. There were also numerous smaller concert-based outreaches throughout the year.

In 2011, I launched my first speaking tour, Murder Your Flesh, accompanied by rap artist The Rep. We drove across the US in an RV, doing nearly forty events in one month. We saw people getting healed and demons being cast out. We prayed for and laid hands on people struggling with AIDS. And through it all, many, many more people were getting saved. The next year I went back out on the road on the War for Your Soul tour. I was traveling something like nine months out of the year. It was a very busy schedule, but I loved it.

Then, out of the blue, came this invitation from Chuck Smith and Brian Brodersen from Calvary Chapel Costa Mesa to start teaching a once-a-month evangelistic Bible study at the church. For all the speaking I had been doing, I'd never taught through the Bible before. I told Bible stories, I quoted Bible verses, I talked about Bible things—but teaching through a book of the Bible was way beyond what I felt comfortable doing. I'd never been to a Bible college. My training came from reading through the Bible four times front to back and spending count-less hours listening to Chuck Smith teach through God's Word verse by verse. So, I knew the Scriptures; I'd just never taught them in a Bible study format. As I prayed through the decision, I recognized the honor it was to teach at the Calvary Chapel mother church, and I figured that Chuck and Brian had to have prayed about it ahead of time. My attitude is if God opens the door, then I'm going to walk on through it. I told them yes.

Prior to that invitation, I used to tell my friends that if I was ever going to teach some sort of study, it would have to be in Orange County. Why? So that I could meet the girl of my dreams. How did I know that my dream girl would live in Orange County? Simple—I was determined not to do long-distance dating. I was over that. I didn't want to drive to LA or Diamond Bar just so I could pick my girl up to take her to dinner. I needed to date someone in my own backyard. So, when God dropped my first teaching gig on me, where was it? Right in the heart of Orange County! That's what's up! God making dreams come true!

By now, you've figured me out well enough to know that if I'm going to do something, I'm going to do it 100 percent and give it my all. After working through a bunch of options, I decided on the name Shine. At the end of each of Chuck Smith's Bible studies, he always pronounced the Aaronic blessing over the listeners. It goes like this:

> The LORD bless you and keep you;
> The LORD make His face shine upon you,
> And be gracious to you;
> The LORD lift up His countenance upon you,
> And give you peace. (Numbers 6:24–26 NKJV)

I love that picture of God's face shining on me. It speaks of His joy in seeing the person I've become. It shows that He is proud of me and sees all that I am doing to serve Him. So, Shine became the name, and I would put those verses up on the screens at the end of every meeting.

We put the word out that this study was going to start. Because people knew the Whosoevers by now and understood the movement's vibe, they knew that it was a place that they could bring their friends. It wasn't going to be cheesy. We weren't going to be speaking Christianese. They figured, "Heck, if it's Ryan and the Whosoevers, I'm inviting some of my buddies with me that don't believe in God."

The first night went really well. It was packed with close to two thousand people. I gave my testimony, the Holy Spirit was moving, and a lot of people got saved—by "saved" I mean that they committed their lives to Jesus Christ. Overall, I figured I'd survived the first one, and I couldn't wait until the next month. After the study was over, I went to the front doors to hang out and to pray with people.

That's when I saw this girl and was like, "Who the heck is that? I mean, WHAT! IS! UP!" I'd traveled the world for twenty years and I'd never seen a girl who looked like that. I was hooked. I couldn't keep my eyes off her. It was like *Dumb and Dumber*—"Oh yeah…tractor beam—sucked me right in."

I was looking at her. Then she looked at me, and our eyes met, and dude…

I was asking around to see if anyone knew her, hoping to get a quick background check on her. Then my brother Raul came over and I asked him, "You know that girl over there?"

Raul said, "Yeah, that's Crystal."

"Crystal? How do you know her?" I was thinking, "Perfect—I've got the 'in.' It's going down now."

"Oh, you've met her before," he told me. "She did some work for our company back in the day."

I'm like, "Trust me: I have never seen this girl before in my life. I would have remembered. Hook me up—introduce me."

So he did, and Crystal and I chopped it up for a little bit, and that was it. I was playing it cool. I didn't want to be some freaky stalker. Besides, there was something I had to learn before I tried to take things any further.

I found this other girl and asked, "Hey, do you know if Crystal is a Christian?"

She said, "No, she's not."

Nooooooo! I'm thinking, "This sucks!" This girl was hot and totally my type and it was all over just like that. THE END! My thought was that if she didn't know Christ, then there wasn't a chance I would be dating her anytime soon. That's not being harsh; that's just keeping it real. Jesus is the Lord of my life. Nobody and nothing can, nor will, be more important than Him. If the most important thing in my life is not the most important thing in her life, then there is no way the relationship could work.

That's why the Bible says that Christians shouldn't marry non-Christians. It isn't because God is being exclusive. It isn't that He's just throwing around random rules to make life harder or to keep us away from all the fun. He knows the way we work. A marriage between a Christian and a non-Christian is always hard, and it's even worse for the kids. God wants us to bring up healthy, happy, godly children, and that won't happen in a home where they're getting mixed messages from their parents about Jesus.

So, I stood there as Crystal walked away. God knows that I didn't want to let her go, but it had to be done. I had to kill the noise that would come from dating a non-Christian girl. I wasn't going to compromise what I believe. Plus, I'd already been there and done that. I wasn't going out like that again.

I didn't see Crystal again for a while. She was living in New York, working for a capital management company. When I had met her, she had been out in Orange County visiting her grandmother, who was very sick.

A couple of months later, though, she surfaced again back at my Bible study. But in that time gap, I had done a little investigating. I had discovered some shady activity of this other girl who had told me that Crystal was not a Christian. So, there was a little bit of hope again that Crystal might yet be *the* girl. But before anything could progress, I needed to get a real answer to whether she was a Christian or not. After the study I made my way in her direction and said, "Hey, why don't you and all your friends and me and all my friends go and grab some food and see what's up?" She agreed and we took off.

Christian dating—LOL! It was kinda weird compared to how I had always dated before. We had a big group around us—everybody was talking and having a good time. It was actually pretty cool. It allowed me to get to know her without any of the pressure. It's a chill atmosphere.

Surrounded by ten people all sitting in one booth, Crystal and I still managed to talk quite a bit. "So, do you go to church?" I asked, worried about the answer I was going to get.

"Yeah, I go to church."

Cool! "How often?" I asked, thinking the answer might be once a week or maybe even twice a week for Bible studies and stuff like that.

"I don't know. I grew up Catholic. Maybe once a month. I'm always there for Christmas and Easter, though."

Ohhhhh! I couldn't believe it. This girl was everything I'd been looking for, but she was only an occasional churchgoer. The more we talked, it became evident that she hadn't received Jesus as her Savior. She didn't have the Holy Spirit in her.

But what I did learn was how much she loved worship music. She listened to Christian radio all the time. She had a real love for God, but she just didn't know how to take that next step of starting a real relationship with Jesus Christ. The power of the Holy Spirit was missing from her life. I wasn't even sure she had ever heard how the Holy Spirit works in our lives.

So, I asked her, "Hey, can I give you a book? It's called *Living Water* by Chuck Smith and it really impacted my life. It's all about the Holy Spirit. I know you're going back to New York this week, so maybe you can just take it with you and read it when you have time."

Crystal agreed to pack it with her. We didn't communicate much while she was across the country. As much as I liked her, I knew I couldn't push her into becoming a Christian. It's up to God to do that work in her life. Besides, who wants to be pushed into anything? Not me—forced relationships are lame.

Meanwhile, God was doing some stuff in her life—shifting things around. He removed her from her job, picked her up, and—what do you know?—planted her back in California.

While waiting for the plane to board to bring her to her new home on the West Coast, she finally opened the Chuck Smith book I had given her. She started reading and immediately got sucked in. Her flight was called, and she kept reading when she got to her seat. God was speaking to her and she couldn't put the book down. There's a place in the book where Pastor Chuck wrote, "If you have not received the Holy Spirit or made that commitment to believe in Jesus Christ, to confess Him as the Lord of your life, I pray that God would speak to your heart right now, before you turn another page."[7] She read that sentence five or six times, and that's when she realized that she didn't have a personal relationship with Jesus Christ. Right there in that airplane seat, she prayed and gave her life to God.

By the time she finished her prayer, she was bawling. Who knows what the person in the seat next to her was thinking? The plane hadn't taken off yet, so Crystal texted me: "Ryan, I read that book and got to the place where it talked about a personal relationship with Christ. I realized I didn't have one. I said a prayer and now I feel love and I'm just crying and I don't know what's going on."

Dude, the way I felt when I read that message—I can't even tell you. I texted her back: "You just got filled with the Holy Spirit and the God of the universe is revealing Himself to you."

She read my text, but before she could respond, the flight attendant told her she had to put her phone on airplane mode. So Crystal had to think about what my text meant for the next six hours as she flew from NYC to LA.

The next day she called me and asked if I wanted to hang out.

Don't have to ask me twice. "Yeah," I said, "what are you thinking?"

"I want to go to church."

Yes! She's becoming a Jesus girl! I thought. I don't think there are six other words in the English language I would have rather heard coming out of her mouth.

We ended up at Calvary San Juan. The pastor, John Randall, was teaching on water baptism—what it means and all that.

Honestly, I wasn't paying attention. I was too hyped on the fact that I was in church with this smoking-hot girl that I'd been dreaming about. My fantasy had become a reality. When Crystal came out of the service, she was shook. She said, "Everything I've known about being a Catholic and getting baptized when I was a baby—it was all meaningless. I need to get baptized again."

"Well, that's funny," I told her. "Just so happens that The Whosoevers are doing our first water baptism at Pirates Cove tomorrow in Newport Beach."

You know, if you aren't following Jesus, then this kind of "perfect timing" seems like crazy luck or a rare coincidence. When you are trusting God to lead your life, then things like this happen all the time—they're par for the course.

After church I took her back to her home. In the car I prayed for her and anointed her with oil. She had to be tripping out at that. I laid my hands on her and prayed that she would get more of the Holy Spirit. The next day she showed up at Pirates Cove and I baptized her. We went from dunking to dating that fast. It doesn't normally work like that, but God has a funny sense of humor.

We started really getting close—and that's when it got crazy. My once-a-month Bible study had turned into once-a-week. God was blessing, people were getting saved and growing, and I was having fun teaching the Bible. I was having great times outside of ministry, too—hanging with my friends, surfing, skating.

Then a division broke out in my study with some of the team. I would see them giving weird looks to Crystal and trash-talking her. Rumors were spreading, and I suddenly felt like I was back in high school. It was a mini soap opera—*As the Bible Study Turns*. The New Testament says, "Among all the parts of the body, the tongue is a flame of fire. It is a whole world of wickedness, corrupting your entire body. It can set your whole life on fire, for it is set on fire by hell itself" (James 3:6). There was a lot of hellfire-setting going on by their tongues.

I pulled my leadership team together and told them, "Listen, there's a division happening here. This is not what God wants. Whoever is with me, then stay with me. But if you're talking trash and spitting poison and telling stories, then I want you and all your friends to leave." After saying that to the team, I said it to the rest of the church. Guess what. No one else left other than the division makers.

It was still very painful because this was Crystal's first experience of this type as a brand-new Christian. The lies and rumors continued to negatively affect my ministry. But as it always happens when we do the hard thing that God asks us to do, He ended up blessing it. My dad was, and still is, pastoring Calvary Chapel Golden Springs. I asked if we could use his church for an additional meeting for Shine. We would continue our weekly study at Costa Mesa, but we would add a Sunday-night study at my dad's church. He agreed, and that new Bible study ended up taking over the Sunday-night service, growing to over a thousand attending weekly. Like Chuck Smith once said, "Blessed are the subtractions, because it means God is doing a new work." Eventually, the service expanded to two nights on two different campuses.

Unfortunately, when the division makers left, they didn't go quietly. They kept talking trash, and the rumors and lies continued to spread to other churches and other people. Then it hit The Whosoevers camp. That was truly devastating.

This storm I was in led me to a dark place, yet I still had peace through it all. I had God and I had Crystal, and I was trusting by faith that God would work out all the details. People I thought I could trust turned out to be untrustworthy, because they were believing the false information they were hearing. I was fasting and praying and in the Word of God constantly, trying to hear God speak so I could make sense of it all. I wanted to figure out what God was doing and what His next move was. Through it all, He kept speaking to me using my studies and the Bible. It was in the midst of seeking God that He gave someone I know a prophetic word for me. This girl had no idea what was going on in my life. She called me up and told me that God was going to replace The Whosoevers team with a new team. She said I shouldn't worry, because God was about to do something new. Turns out that was exactly what happened. Very quickly, the Lord replaced them all.

Despite God's encouragement through that vision, it was still a very difficult time. I struggled to manage my emotions at times, trying to keep anger and bitterness away from my heart. The only thing that kept me on point was going to God daily and asking His forgiveness for when I let my emotions get the better of me. I would ask Him to change my heart and mind so that I could be used by Him, rather than giving the devil a victory by allowing him a stronghold in my life and ministry. Thankfully, while all this was going on, back on the home front Sonny and Head had my back and were supportive. They continued to tour with their bands but were praying for me and for the ministry while I tried to keep things together at the home base.

It was a huge relief once the division makers had left The Whosoevers. But then my buddy Nick pulled me aside and told me that he was leaving, too. God had chosen that particular time to lead him away from The Whosoevers to start cutting hair. He hoped that maybe he'd even be able to open his own barbershop. That totally sucked. He was the director of operations for the movement and the only one I trusted at that point. I was thinking, "Really, God? This is really the time for him to go?" I was really bummed out, but I also didn't want to hold Nick back from what God was calling him to do. The last thing I'd ever want to do is get in the way of God's plans for someone. I just said, "All right, dude, go get it."

It was pretty cool to watch Nick. Like I said before, when God calls us to something, He will always give us the grace we need to carry it out. After a few years of going to school and getting his training, Nick opened up his shop and it's pretty awesome. You looking for a good fade? Go see my boy Nick!

The division had shaken up the movement and had reached into my family. What made that so hard was that it all centered around Crystal. I had finally found the woman that I knew God had brought to me, and everyone I knew and loved seemed to be either lying and spreading rumors about her or buying into the lies and rumors. Many of my team from the Shine study and The Whosoevers who I used to kick it with daily were no longer around. But all the while, God was working and moving things—setting me up for His next session for my life and taking me deeper in the study of His Word so I would be ready for His lead.

God is faithful. Never forget that. God is faithful—every time, all the time. In the middle of the storm, He showed up. He gave me that word of prophecy from that girl, and I trusted that the Holy Spirit was going to come through. I was nervous—maybe even a bit scared—but I sat back and waited to see what God would do. By "sat back" I don't mean that I just chilled on my couch with an Animal Style Double-Double and a chocolate shake from In-N-Out, even though that's a great way to live. I kept on with my fasting and praying and digging into the Word. I didn't know what God was going to do, but I knew He was going to do something—and I wanted to be ready when He did it.

God moved! First, as I mentioned earlier, God replaced The Whosoevers team overnight. He filled all those empty chairs in the movement's office with amazing people. Second, the Shine study—my weekly Bible study—spread from Orange County up to my dad's church in Diamond Bar, a city east of Los Angeles. And third, all the while, God began really making it clear that Crystal was going to be my wife. When I was in this very dark place in my life, God showed up and—one, two, three— He did something beautiful three times in a row. The best part about it is that it was all God. I had no control—not of anything. I just knew that I had to keep doing what He had called me to do, and that He would take care of the rest.

And just when I thought that God couldn't be any more amazing than He'd already been, He took it to the next level. I was at a dinner for my birthday and Crystal gave me a card. I read through it, and when I got to the end, my jaw dropped. Seriously, I was tripping out. At the bottom of the card she had written out a verse: "The eyes of the LORD search the whole earth in order to strengthen those whose hearts are fully committed to him" (2 Chronicles 16:9). If you're thinking, "Dude, what's the big deal? It's just a verse," then check this out.

Remember, this was still in the storm while things were just starting to come together. I was sure that this was the girl God wanted me to marry, but everyone was telling me, "Don't do it. Stay away from her." There were people who were actually praying that God would split us apart—think about how crazy that is. At some point you have to start asking yourself, "Am I the one who is crazy? Has love blinded me so that I'm acting like a fool?" But then Crystal wrote that verse—that epic, random verse.

Looking up from the card, I asked her, "Where did you get that verse from? You've only been a Christian for a few weeks. You've been to church, like, five or six times. Our Bible study is going through the Gospel of Mark. You have no business knowing anything about the Old Testament book of Chronicles! Where in the heck did you find this verse?"

She looked at me like I was crazy. "I googled 'encouraging verses,' and there were something like sixty that popped up on my screen. I read over them and this was the one that kept popping off the page, so I put it in the card. What's the problem?"

I told her, "Look, five years ago in 2008, I bought my first iPhone. When I brought it home, I tried out the sticky note app by writing out my life verse. It's the only sticky note I've written in five years of having that phone." I pulled out my phone, opened the app, and showed her—"The eyes of the LORD search the whole earth in order to strengthen those whose hearts are fully committed to him" (2 Chronicles 16:9).

Do you know the chances of her choosing my life verse? There are over thirty-one thousand verses in the Bible. For her to pick that one verse—either I've got really good luck or God is real and He's in all the details of our lives. I said to her, "Hey, we need to talk about getting married." And she said, "Yes."

In case there is still anyone out there doubting God's hand in bringing Crystal and me together, let me tell you just a little more of the story. When I was in second grade, my mom was driving me home from school. For some reason we were talking about getting married. I told her that I already knew the name of the girl I wanted to marry—Crystal. I'm not sure why I said that—maybe it was because I liked the way crystals looked when I was young.

Fast-forward quite a few years to a day when I'm thinking about the type of girl I want to marry. I actually came up with a list. I love brightly colored eyes. I dig dark hair. I love me some Latina girls with olive skin, like the ones who live anywhere from Mexico to South America, because I'd grown up traveling throughout South America. And I was determined not to even start dating a girl who lived more than fifteen minutes from my house. That's Laguna Beach to San Clemente to Huntington. Driving in Southern California is the worst—I was too old for a long-distance relationship, taking daily drives from Orange County up to Ventura or Camarillo or Oxnard.

So, who does God send me? He sends me a girl whose name is Crystal. Her family is half Swiss/German and half

Argentine—and she definitely favors the Argentine side. She has beautiful dark hair and perfect olive skin. And she has one and a half blue eyes. That's right—one full blue, and the other split right down the middle with one half blue and the other half 50 percent green and 50 percent brown. God didn't just give me color—He gave me all the colors! Oh yeah, and when I met her, she was living in Dana Point, which was exactly fifteen minutes from my house. As I said, either I have really good luck or God is real and He's involved in the details of our lives.

In Matthew 9, Jesus talked about wineskins. A wineskin, made out of animal hide, is what they used as bottles before there were bottles. If you use an old, patched wineskin to hold new wine, the pressure from the new stuff will burst it and you will lose both the wine and the wineskin. Jesus used this fact to illustrate the new covenant and the new religious system that were going to come in because of His death on the cross. He said, "You can't put the Gospel of salvation through My death on the cross into the old wineskins of the law and the current religious system. You need the new wineskins of grace and faith."

This "new wine into new wineskins" is what it felt like God was doing with The Whosoevers. God wanted to open the door to a whole new way to reach people through the movement, but it wasn't going to fit in our old ways. The people of that first generation of ministry worked very hard and helped pioneer the birth of The Whosoevers. We did it all side by side. But to do what God wanted to do next, He needed to remove the old wineskins—the old way of doing things—and pour these new opportunities into a whole new outreach structure. Removing the old is almost always painful, and the storms God took me and The Whosoevers through were no exception. But it had to be done.

It's easy to keep doing things the way you've always done them. The problem with that is God is always moving. If you aren't in tune with where He wants to move you, you will get stuck in a ministry rut. Chuck Smith has had a big impact on my life, so I will quote him again. He said, "The only difference between a rut and a grave is the depth and the width."[8]

Once the new team was together, we began brainstorming and praying and fasting to see what God wanted to do next. We asked the very basic question, why do we even exist? What is the whole purpose of the movement? We determined that, quite simply, it's to get the Gospel to the next generation—students. And where are the students? Well, obviously, they're in schools. Okay, so how do we get into schools?

We started asking around, and the people we talked to said that you can't go into schools and preach the Gospel—it's just not allowed. We took their word for it, and started trying to come up with an alternative. Soon we found that after school there seemed to be a whole different set of rules. So, we started putting on after-school events, and kids were showing up and getting saved. The problem was that it cost a lot for the production we needed. We also realized that a majority of the students were taking off right after school. They just wanted to get home or go smoke weed and drink like I did when I was in school. We had to find a way to get to them while they were still on campus.

One day I got asked by some of my friends from another Calvary Chapel campus to speak at a high school lunchtime assembly in the gymnasium. I told them that I thought we couldn't do that, but they're like, "Well, we're doing it." I was like, "No way! That's awesome!" They gave me the mic and I preached the Gospel. As a result, 98 percent of the kids left their seats in the bleachers and came down to the gym floor. I was shocked, because I'd never seen that happen at public events before. They circled up and right there during lunchtime on a high school campus they repented and asked Jesus into their hearts. That started a whole new way of reaching students. From the time we launched this new "lunch in the gym" outreach up until 2019, we've seen over seventy-five thousand middle schoolers and high schoolers give their lives to Christ. Again, this is during school hours over just the last four years. I believe this is only the beginning of what God has planned.

Time went by and one day I got a phone call from my friend. This friend, who was a big-time radio host, said, "Hey, the station director wants to meet with you for lunch about some radio stuff." I said, "Cool. I'll be there." I was stoked for the meeting because I always had wanted to do a radio show. I'd been on his talk show a few times, being interviewed or promoting events. I remember thinking, "Man, I'd love to host a show like this. You get to hang out and talk to really cool people. That'd be totally rad." Problem was I had no expertise, no qualifications, no training. It was just a dream.

What happened next is so typical of how God works with me. Every time I'd get invited to do something, I'd have no qualifications. I had no qualifications for teaching a Bible study—I'd never been to a Bible college or seminary. I had no qualifications for leading assemblies at schools. I had no qualifications for doing a radio show. But I didn't need qualifications.

Jesus is the Lord of my life and He has the keys to every door that He wants me to walk through. I am led by the Holy Spirit. Jesus said to not worry when you're wanting to talk about Him but you're not sure what to say. "I'll send you the Holy Spirit," He said, "and He'll give you all the words you need." And that's exactly what He did with me. All He was looking for from me was a yes; then He took it from there.

I met with some of the staff of the radio station. They said to me, "Okay, Ryan, you're here because we want to get some younger guys on our station. We see you working with young people, and you really seem to have a voice to that generation." I'm thinking, "Yeah, I like where this is going." They continued, "We want to give you a radio show."

"I like it," I said, playing it cool. "How long would the show be?"

"Maybe thirty minutes. Maybe an hour."

I was sitting there thinking, "Is this really happening?" I asked, "Interesting. What kind of show are you thinking of? Teaching or something like that?"

"Ryan, you can make it whatever you want."

"Well, I think a talk show would be sick."

They looked at each other, then back at me, then said, "Okay, it's yours. Nine to ten on Saturday nights. What do you think?"

"Let's do it!" We shook hands and I headed out the door. But when I got outside, I stopped. "What did I just commit to? This is nuts! I'm crazy! I know nothing about hosting a radio talk show. It's so crazy that it has to be a God thing!" Again, God opens the door and all He's looking for is a yes.

After I left, I went to another meeting I already had lined up.

Coincidentally enough, it was at a different radio station. I was connecting with Brian Brodersen, now the owner of KWAVE studios, to talk with him about a tour I was doing. We met and talked about ministry. Then, when I was leaving, I stopped and turned around. "Hey, Brian, have you guys ever thought about doing a talk show where you interview different musicians and artists and maybe take calls? Kind of like a Jesus 101 with a lot of what's going on in the culture thrown in."

Brian said, "You know what? We've been literally talking about this for months. Why?"

I felt that God was moving. There are no coincidences. "It's like this—I just got offered a radio show up in LA with another station. The thing is I don't want to drive up there every week. It'll take me at least a solid hour each way, and that's without traffic. Honestly, it would be so much better if I could just do it out of your studio." I was thinking that maybe I could do the show at KWAVE, then send the recording up to the other station.

"Yeah, we'll do it," Brian said. "I'll give you nine to ten on Saturday nights."

God shows up again. He's just looking for a yes.

"Okay, sick. Thanks for the opportunity. We'll talk soon," I said to him as I headed out. But as I left, it hit me—"Oh my gosh, that's the same time I already committed to. Am I going to have to pick one or the other?" So, I got to my car and I prayed, and the thought hit me: "Why don't you ask if you can do the show out of KWAVE in Orange County and see if the other station can pick up the feed?"

I called KWAVE up and they said, "Sure, Ryan, we'll do it. Wouldn't be any extra work for us. But getting the other station to pick up the feed from us is going to be like Moses parting the Red Sea, because radio stations just don't do that. Good luck."

So, I started thinking about how I could pitch this to the other station. I developed this whole plan about how this would be so much better for everyone and how it would reach such a wide audience. I practiced my little speech a few times until I got it down; then I picked up the phone.

"Hey, so I got an idea. I live down in Orange County, and for a fifteen-minute drive I could just go to KWAVE and you guys could pick up the feed weekly."

"Yeah, Ryan. No problem. We'll do it."

Just like that? No begging or pleading or convincing? I've got my whole pitch ready—can't I take just a little time to sell it?

That's the way God does it. It's that blessing that God gives to those who are ready to say yes no matter what. I was in the storm with people trash-talking me and God was opening up all these huge doors. Without the storm, I wouldn't have been looking around for new opportunities.

It all started with a yes to teaching a Bible study. The study allowed me to meet my future wife. Meeting my future wife led to division. The division led to bringing in a new team. Bringing in a new team led to school tours, leading to thousands of teens getting saved. Meanwhile, the Bible study grew to two nights a week. A radio show was born with two stations, and now it has blown up to 114 stations from LA to New York City. It's the Holy Spirit working step by step to accomplish His will. Looking back now, I can see the progression. In the middle of it, though, I didn't know what the heck was going on. Each day was another step of faith.

As we show our faith in God, He is always faithful to us.

Again, I don't qualify for any of the great ministry stuff God was and is doing through me. But God uses ordinary people to do extraordinary things. I can't tell you how many times early on I left the radio station expecting a call on the way home saying, "Well, Ryan, it was a good run, but you're just not cut out for radio." Or I'd finish a Bible study thinking I'd end up getting told, "Please, Ryan, no more."

Maybe one day it will happen. In the meantime, you know what God wants from me? He wants me to show up. He wants me to just say yes, walk through the door, and let Him take it from there.

CHAPTER 9

Living the Impossible

As I mentioned earlier, I am under a stay-at-home order from the California governor because of COVID-19, or the novel coronavirus. When this book is published, perhaps we will all know the full extent of the pandemic. We will know how many lives this virus has taken. We will know what all the preventative measures have done to our economy. So many of the questions that I and the rest of the world have right at this moment will hopefully have answers. But for now, as I look into the future, I see a whole lot of unknowns.

Take yourself back to April 2020, and again, it's madness. People are panicking, buying up all the toilet paper and hand sanitizer they can find. Grocery store shelves are empty by the end of each selling day. Over two million guns have been sold recently across the country, and all the gun stores in California are out of ammo. Businesses are closing in order to keep social distancing, churches across the nation are doing their services online, and our governor here in California just shut down all the beaches.

But even in the midst of the craziness, there are great things happening, too. My friend Ally Brooke just hit number one on the dance music charts with "All Night," an Afrojack song that she collaborated on. My boys, Islander, dropped their cover of R.E.M.'s "It's the End of the World as We Know It." My wife has decided to fulfill her lifelong passion to be an entrepreneur and is starting a vitamin company called American Made Naturals. I've even had the chance to launch a new business—Custom Branded—where we design and produce custom footwear and apparel for different companies. So there is some silver lining in the midst of this storm. There always is—you just have to look for it.

Overall, though, it is just madness. Just two weeks ago I canceled a Kill the Noise tour in Chile because of travel restrictions. That was a bummer losing that chance to take the Gospel to South America. Can you remember the fear during that time? You may be reading this thinking, "Oh, Ryan, you are so naïve. You have no idea yet just how bad it's about to get." Or you may be shaking your head, saying, "Dude, this thing ended up so overblown that it's hard to remember why everyone was freaking out."

The future of this virus is a huge black hole for me living in April 2020. I wish past-me could know now what future-you knows as you're reading this chapter. But I'm not stressing. That lack of knowledge may be frustrating, but it isn't frightening. I'd like the answers, but I don't need to have them for there to be peace in my heart. My peace comes not from what I know, but from Who I know.

There are three ways to live in this life. The first looks at an unknown future and is scared to death. People who live this way realize that, ultimately, they are just victims of circumstances. They may work out every day of their lives, so they're totally shredded. They may load themselves up with supplements and vitamins and eat vegan and gluten-free—anything to make their life last longer. But they also recognize that regardless of their best efforts, one day a virus can come along and take them out. Or, they could just walk out of the gym and get run over by a bus. This terrifies them. The Bible talks about people like this being "slaves to the fear of dying" (Hebrews 2:15).

The second way to live is to ignore the future. Because they don't know what might happen tomorrow, people who live this way ignore the possibility of a virus or a bus taking them out. They pretend like tomorrow will never come and bad things will never happen. Like King Solomon wrote, "There is nothing better for people in this world than to eat, drink, and enjoy life" (Ecclesiastes 8:15). Who wants to think about tomorrow when there's a party going on today? People used to call this "whistling past the graveyard." You're walking next to a cemetery filled with dead people. But since you're scared to face the unknowns of death, you look the other way and whistle yourself some happy little song. That may work until you get cancer or the virus starts working on your lungs or you and the bus become intimately acquainted at forty miles an hour, and you suddenly realize that it's too late to think about the future because you have no more future.

The third way is to live a life trusting in the God who is bigger than what's going on around you. It recognizes that giving control of our lives to the Ultimate Power of the universe who can do the impossible just makes sense. He has the strength and the authority to stop the bus or kill the virus. On top of that, He loves us and has promised that He will always do what is best for us. That's a guarantee—He does not lie. Sometimes this means protecting us from the struggle. Sometimes it means walking through the struggle alongside us. Sometimes it means letting the struggle take our lives. In any of those situations, if we have given ourselves to Jesus and let the Holy Spirit fill us with His peace, then we have nothing to worry about.

I've lived life each of these ways at different times in my life. I've been scared of the future when I've seen my buddies overdose and die. I lived a lot of years just not thinking about tomorrow—using drugs and sleeping with girls and drinking alcohol to numb my brain so I didn't have to think about what would happen if my plane went down or if the mix of cocaine, pills, and alcohol finally collapsed my system. Neither of those first two ways was good. They were both based completely on the fear of dealing with the truth.

But now I'm living the third way—the way of hope. I'm trusting God for everything—my future, my family, The Whosoevers Movement. Living this way is so much better. I don't have to have fear in my life anymore. I don't need to be worried about the future—the viruses, the busses, and just the everyday problems that are always there in life. Of course, that doesn't mean I don't use common sense, wisdom, and the brain that God gave me to keep myself from getting into stupid or dangerous situations. But I know that when times are tough, God will do whatever is best for me and my family—even if it means doing the impossible. Sometimes He'll work through the natural, and sometimes He'll do the miraculous. How do I know this? Because I've seen Him do it in my life over and over and over. With God there is always hope, and with His hope comes peace.

God was expanding The Whosoevers Movement. Through His power and plan, we were reaching people all around the world with the truth about Jesus and the eternal life that comes through a relationship with Him. All the craziness of the attacks and the divisions of years past had settled down. Life was good.

About a year after we were married, Crystal said she wanted to talk. After we sat down, she told me that if we were going to have kids, now would be the time. I'm eight years older than she is, and she wanted to make sure that we were young enough to really enjoy a family. When she said that, I thought, "That's cool. I mean, I'm fine either way. Life is great as it is, but I wouldn't mind having a little mini-me around. Besides, I'm not getting any younger. I don't want to end up looking like a grandpa with a kid!" So we decided we'd try for a baby.

First month—no pregnancy. No big deal. Second month—no pregnancy. Again, no sweat. Sometimes it takes a little while. Third month, fourth month, fifth month—still nothing. Eventually, we passed the year mark, and then the two-year mark. Still no pregnancy.

For those who have not had to deal with infertility, it's hard to understand the emotional toll that it can take. Crystal, especially, felt the struggle. Every month when it becomes obvious that there is no pregnancy, it's almost like a new stress and pain process starts again. I could see the beginnings of real anxiety in Crystal. Depression was creeping in. Not a "lock yourself in a room and you won't come out" kind of depression. Crystal's not that kind of girl, and I'm not that kind of guy. But still, it weighs on you—month after month after month.

Eventually, you start questioning whether it will ever happen. You begin speculating through all the what-ifs: What if we can never have kids? What if it's physically my fault, and I'm the reason my wife will never be able to experience what it's like to have a baby and be a mom? It gets weird for sure. With each passing month, there's disappointment. By the time the second year had passed, I could see the real pain that Crystal felt.

We started acupuncture sessions with Dr. Kevin Huang at Agape Natural Health in Newport Beach to get "our bodies tuned up," as he would say. Then we had our fertility doc check us both out, and we discovered that Crystal had endometriosis—a condition that would likely be responsible for keeping her from getting pregnant. That was a frustrating diagnosis. This was one of those "What the heck is going on, God?" moments. We weren't mad at Him. We just couldn't figure out why things were going down like they were. So, we just said, "Okay, God, You've got Your reasons. We're going to trust You and just keep riding this thing out." As much of a bummer as it was to get the diagnosis of Crystal's endometriosis, it was great to finally have an answer. Crystal had surgery, and suddenly we were back in the game. But the months passed, and still no pregnancy.

We decided we'd head back to the docs, but this time to

ones who are there specially to help couples struggling like we were. They tested us and gave us good news and bad news. The good news was that there was nothing wrong with us, and they had no idea why we weren't getting pregnant. The bad news was there was nothing wrong with us, and they had absolutely no idea why we weren't getting pregnant.

We were in the storm once again. When you really want something and the something that you want really seems like it would be such a good thing, it's tough letting go of it and saying, "God, this is Yours. You do what You're going to do." However, when you are able to put whatever you're facing in God's hands and say, "Your will be done," there is a huge peace that comes. And with that peace is a hope that because of His deep love for you, you know He will work it out for the best, one way or another.

I've seen couples who never get to that place. Not being able to have kids takes over their lives. Marriages get destroyed because of how fixated the husband and wife become on having a baby. It becomes an idol or a god to them. They worship at the feet of parenthood. And when their god ends up letting them down, depression and resentment set in. So often, those marriages end up in divorce. Crystal and I were dedicated to never letting that happen to us. We weren't going to go out like that.

Trusting God's will didn't mean that we were giving up. It just meant that we were going to accept whatever God's outcome would be. We decided to check out some fertility specialists. They took us through some procedures, but still nothing. So we said, "Okay, God, whatever You decide, we're cool. Our last shot is going to be trying one round of this expensive in vitro fertilization. If it works, great. If not, we're done." We were not going to let this become an idol.

We went through the process, then waited. What was God going to do? Remember, with faith you can be sure that whatever God decides will turn out to be epic. He knows what's best.

Then, after waiting for what seemed like forever, we got a call from the doc. He said, "So, looks like you guys are going to be parents." We were in shock. God did it! We were freaking out. Thank you, Jesus!

The doctor said we needed to come in, so I took Crystal to get checked out. That's when the doctor dropped more information on us. "So, there's a second baby." I was like, "What the heck! No way!" He said, "Yup, fraternal twins. Healthy as anything—at least for now."

"Wait. At least for now? What does that mean?" we asked the doctor.

"Because of Crystal's past medical issues, this is a very high-risk pregnancy. I need to see you back here every two weeks so we can closely monitor these babies. You guys aren't in the clear, but so far the babies look healthy."

That caused a little concern, but we figured that if God had brought us this far, He could take us the rest of the way. We called up the family and told them the amazing news: "Hey, guess what—we're having twins." Everybody was praising God. My dad was like, "No way! You're messing with me." I started laughing. "Yeah, it's happening!"

Two weeks later, we were back for a checkup. Crystal was getting an ultrasound, and everything looked great. The babies were growing and their heartbeats were strong. I was watching the ultrasound's monitor, getting more and more excited as I saw the flutter of my little twins' hearts pumping away. Then I cracked a joke: "Oh my gosh, Doctor, what is that?" I said, pointing at the screen. Crystal was not amused by the joke.

But then the doctor looked and said, "Uh, I think there's another one in there."

"Shut up!" I said as I moved closer to the screen.

"No, seriously," he replied as he moved the probe over to the other side of Crystal's stomach. He turned the volume up on the ultrasound and we heard this new fast little heartbeat. Crystal and I just looked at each other, like deer in headlights. We were totally in shock—like twilight zone kind of shock. We asked the doc how this was even possible.

"One of the eggs split a week late. Your twins are now triplets." He continued, "Unfortunately, this looks like it could very well end up being a vanishing twin scenario. With this late of a split the new twin rarely makes it. Babies A and B are healthy and strong. The new twin, Baby C, looks like it's struggling. Come back in two weeks and we'll see if this new baby can catch up." The doctor didn't even give us an ultrasound picture of Baby C.

So we left and immediately started sharing the news. "Hey, guys, we have some crazy news. One of the eggs split and we're having triplets. I mean, is this nuts or what? I'm tripping!" Again, everyone started freaking out. My dad tells me, "Now I really know you're messing with me."

After the excitement died down, we let them know the prognosis for the third baby. "Guys, we really need to pray, because the doc said that Baby C is most likely not going to catch up. It's just too far behind in development." That's when it really kicked in. We were so happy and felt so much appreciation over the gifts that God had given to us. But that happiness was muted, kind of distant—like you don't want to get too excited because it might all come crashing down at any moment. Once again, we held on to the promise that if God had taken us this far, He was going to take us all the way.

Now we were in the storm. We had two babies that were in a high-risk pregnancy and a newly discovered third baby who probably wasn't going to make it. We needed peace, so we prayed. That's how you tap into God's peace. You just ask Him. You have not because you ask not. The Bible says, "Don't worry about anything; instead, pray about everything. Tell God what you need, and thank him for all he has done. Then you will experience God's peace, which exceeds anything we can understand. His peace will guard your hearts and minds as you live in Christ Jesus" (Philippians 4:6–7). It's a promise directly from God to us. You're worried? Bring your problem to Me. Let Me take care of it. Hand it over to Me, and I'll replace it with perfect peace.

So, we prayed. Our family prayed. Our friends prayed. Our church prayed. People we'd never even met prayed. It even became a big deal online with thousands praying around the world. It's through these prayers that the confidence of "Lord, Your will be done" entered our hearts and our minds. We knew that God was in control, and He will always do what is best for us, for those babies, and especially for that tiny Baby C.

It was a long two weeks waiting until our next appointment. When it finally came, Crystal lay back on the exam table and the nurse fired up the ultrasound. Both Crystal and I were praying silently as the doctor started searching for the babies with his ultrasound wand. Then came the report. "Surprisingly, Baby C is catching up with the other two."

For the second time in two weeks, we freaked out. It was a mixture of "God, we can't believe You just came through like that" and "God, we knew You could do it."

"But…" came the doctor's voice.

I really didn't want to hear that "but." In fact, I was very happy without the "but." I was thinking, "Okay, Doc, how about you just clean this ultrasound goop from Crystal's stomach; then we'll walk out, and you can keep your 'but' to yourself." Before I could communicate to him what I thought to be a very sensible plan, he continued.

"But your high-risk pregnancy is now a very high-risk pregnancy. First of all, Crystal's life could be in danger, because she is carrying three babies. Second, while Baby C is catching up, there's still a ways to go. Finally, Baby A is already sitting very low and could cause premature labor. You need to understand that there are a lot of different things that could happen, a lot of different scenarios—most of them are not good. We're going to need to monitor you guys extremely closely."

The storm was ramping up—the wind was howling and the waves were crashing. This situation was really serious. We weren't talking about financial problems or The Whosoevers or church division. We were talking life and death. I let the listeners of my radio show know what was going on and asked them to pray. We got other prayer warriors praying, and we kept going back to see the doctor. At each appointment, we would get the report that the babies just kept growing. We were thinking that maybe God was going to smooth-sail us through this storm. Then we got to sixteen weeks, and a wave hit our boat, tossing us around until we landed hard on the deck with the wind knocked out of us.

The doctor sat us down after the examination and said, "I'm sorry to tell you this. Crystal, your cervix is giving out. Holding in three babies has just become too much. These babies are literally one millimeter from coming out, and if they don't stay in for at least a few months more, they are not going to live. They just wouldn't be developed enough to survive on the outside. Even if they do somehow stay in a few more months, they'll likely end up being born with major health problems. However, I don't think you need to concern yourself with future health problems. I just don't see any way that they'll be able to make it that far."

———

The New Testament tells the story of a lady who had been bleeding for twelve years. We don't know the cause or what exactly her suffering looked like. We just know that she was miserable. She had spent all of her money on doctors and medicine, but nobody and nothing could help her. She had lost hope.

That's where we suddenly found ourselves. It had been one storm after another, and now we were losing hope. No medicine, no money, no doctors could do what was needed to keep these babies in. They're a millimeter from coming out and dying. One millimeter! Get yourself a ruler and take a look at how tiny a millimeter is. That's all there was between our triplets living and dying. The doctor told us to keep coming back until the babies passed, just so they could make sure that Crystal survived okay. And that was it. The verdict was in and the sentence was read—death. We sat there trying to process what he was saying.

That bleeding woman had no hope. But then she heard about Jesus—this healing prophet. Suddenly, there was a little spark of hope. Maybe, if she could just see Him, touch Him—maybe not all was lost. So she went to find Jesus. She found Him. She had faith in Him. She touched Him. Healing came. Hope returned. Her life changed forever.

If all we had was the word of the doctor, we would have been hopeless. Three little babies gone at once—it was more than we could handle. The storm was extremely dark and dangerous. But like the woman, we had faith beyond medicine and doctors. We went looking for Jesus and His healing. Crystal and I prayed, "Jesus, You know our hearts. You know our love for these babies. But we know Your love for them also. These babies are Yours and You can do whatever You want with them. If You want them, You can have them. But as for us, we want life. So, here we are, God, and we're praying for life. Yet more than anything else, we want Your will to be done." It was after this prayer that we gave our future daughters the middle names Hope, Faith, and Grace. Our daily prayer to God was, "By Faith, we have Hope in You that You will show Grace to these girls."

That first night after our appointment, God woke my mom up at three o'clock in the morning and gave her a vision. She wrote it out and emailed it to me the next day. She said that in her vision there was a boat that looked like it was from the New Testament times. It was in a huge storm on the sea. At the front looking forward into the wind and rain was a brown-haired baby girl. Below her were identical twin girls sleeping soundly through the wind and waves. As my mom watched, the boat began to transform. The wood morphed into skin, the boards into fingers. That's when she recognized what had happened. The boat had become the hands of Jesus. My mom wrote that God had shown her that the babies were in a difficult storm, but Jesus had them safely in His hands. That was such a comfort, because we knew that all signs and wonders point back to the truth that Jesus is the Messiah and that the Word of God is real.

Not long after, we received another vision from a friend. She told us that she had seen three small coffins. Written on each coffin was the word "fear." As she watched, Jesus came along, took a rag, and wiped "fear" off of each little wooden coffin. God was telling us to trust Him. He knew the circumstances, and He was working.

Our next step was to find a pregnancy specialist who deals with multiples that are trying to come out too early. God led us to a doctor in Irvine, California. I remember how I felt walking into his office. I knew God was leading us, I knew He had it under control, but I just needed a sign. There's nothing wrong with telling God, "I just need a little something—a little encouragement to know I'm on the right path." In the Old Testament, Gideon asked for one sign after another—"God, burn up this food" (Judges 6:17–21); "God, make the fleece wet and the ground dry" (Judges 6:36–38); "God, make the ground wet and the fleece dry" (Judges 6:39–40); "Gideon, I know you're still doubting—here's one more sign" (Judges 7:9–15). Each time, God willingly gave Gideon the boost he needed. God knows that faith isn't always easy. When we need a reminder that He's there, He'll often give it to us.

Dr. Kurtzman called us in and we started making small talk, getting to know each other. The doctor asked us what we do for a living. I told him about The Whosoevers—how I speak and do a radio show. A big smile spread across his face as he listened. He said, "That's fantastic. My wife, Jeannine, and I are Christians." We started talking about God and inside I was saying, "Yeah, God, this is You working."

After checking out Crystal, the doctor laid out the prognosis in a way that took both medicine and faith into consideration. He said, "It's true that according to the world, there is essentially no hope. But our hope is in Christ."

After that appointment, Crystal was put on extreme bed rest. And we're talking extreme! She could take a shower every couple of days just for hygiene. No cooking, no getting out of bed. She had to spend day in and day out lying down with her hips up. At this point it was all about gravity. Crystal's acupuncture doctor, Dr. Kevin, who had also been praying and loving us through this journey, laid out the scary reality of our situation. She had to listen closely to her doctors and play it safe.

The weeks and months went on. Then the storm meter went up another level. Baby C wasn't getting enough food. Dr. Kurtzman said that we might need to take the baby out early, because it could be life-threatening for her. But if any of the babies were to come out at that point in development, they would inevitably have major health complications, because their lungs wouldn't be fully developed. So, we continued our prayer of "God, not our will but Your will be done."

The weeks passed and God miraculously kept feeding those babies and keeping them safe where they belonged. Then the day finally came when the three of them were done waiting.

They were ready to see the outside world. "It's getting way too cramped, so we're out of here!" Out they came—eight months into the pregnancy! That's four months after the doctors said it was impossible to keep them in anymore. Four months after hearing that there was no way these little girls would survive. Now, here we were, looking at healthy triplet daughters— Sadielyn Grace, Lillian Faith, and Evelyn Hope. They were small, and each of them spent a little time in the NICU (neonatal intensive care unit). But God had carried them through.

Dude, it is amazing being a father. The first time I held those girls and looked into their eyes and had their tiny hands grip my finger—that was when I really started to understand the incredible love of God. I would do anything for my girls, and there is nothing in this world that brings me as much joy as they do. If I, as a flawed person and an imperfect father, can have such a deep love for my children, how much greater must our perfect heavenly Father's love for us be.

It wasn't until later, after the storm had passed, that I began putting a few things together in my mind. Before this intense trial, I had been trying to block out everything that had occurred with my previous relationship. There were not a lot of great memories there. But the pregnancy had flipped a switch in my brain, and my internal hard drive started downloading all this stuff from my earlier life. It was then that I realized how the Lord had shown me the difference between going through life with God and without God.

When I had no faith and was living for myself by going after my body appetites, I had a chance to be a father. But sin was in my life and in my girlfriend's life. There was no Bible to lay a foundation of morality. We had no God to turn to for wisdom.

So that first child, that beautiful gift of life, was aborted. One baby gone.

Then my girlfriend and I got pregnant again. We straightened ourselves out so we could be good parents to this new little life, but we tried it on our own. There was still no God in the picture. Then the doctor told us that the egg split late and there were twins—so awesome! But he immediately followed with the news that the new twin had died—so devastating! Just that fast, joy turned to sorrow. Then came the call from my girlfriend saying that she just wasn't ready to be a mom, so she aborted the surviving baby. Over the course of our relationship, three babies were gone—two aborted and one a vanishing twin.

A long time ago there was a prophet named Joel. In the short Old Testament book that he wrote, he talked about the punishment that God was going to bring on Israel for their disobedience. Locusts were coming and life was about to get crazy. These grasshopper-type bugs have enormous appetites, and they fly around in swarms that number in the millions. They'll sweep in and wipe out hundreds of acres of wheat and grain at a time. Through Joel, God told the Israelites that He was doing this to wake them up from their sins so they would turn to Him.

While that may seem harsh, what's beautiful is His promise to them for when they finally turn away from their idol worship and chasing after their body appetites. He promised restoration—a return to a relationship with Him and a replacement for what sin had taken from them. God said to them, "And I will restore to you the years that the locust hath eaten, the cankerworm, and the caterpillar, and the palmerworm, my great army which I sent among you. And ye shall eat in plenty, and be satisfied, and praise the name of the LORD your God, that hath dealt wondrously with you: and my people shall never be ashamed" (Joel 2:25–26 KJV). In my rebellion against God, I lost three children in two pregnancies. When I repented and returned to God, He restored to me all three in one pregnancy.

Now God is allowing me to tour around the world and tell this story. It's an example of His love, grace, and faithfulness, and He is using it to lead thousands of teens and adults to the Lord. In a sense, this is my story. But much more so, it is a story about God.

After the girls were born, I didn't plan on having more kids. It's really crazy raising triplets. Think about it—the terrible twos times three, diapers times three, teething times three, potty training times three. They're amazing kids—it's just that it can get really intense. There are a lot of wild moments, and you can multiply them all by three.

But for a solid year, Crystal felt like the Holy Spirit was telling her that He wanted to give her a son. And He was very clear that it wasn't just another child, but very specifically a boy. This was pretty crazy, because over the previous few years God had been sending me the same word from other sources. Twelve people from different places around the world had told me, "I had a dream that you had a boy." I'd say, "No way; it's too crazy right now."

So then Crystal hits me up with it one day, and I tell her, "Uh, no way! That's crazy!" First off, we have three under three and that is hectic already. Plus, we live very active lives, and I have a pretty busy travel schedule with tours and speaking. But the main problem was with how risky her last pregnancy was. I wasn't sure we wanted to take a chance with another.

She was sure that this was what the Holy Spirit was telling her. But I wasn't hearing anything. I told her, "God is going to have to send lightning from the sky to tell me He wants us to have another baby." This difference of views carried on for a number of months, and still I hadn't heard anything from God.

Finally we came to a point where a decision had to be made. I told Crystal that I needed to hear from God, and I was heading out to the desert. Anytime I need an answer to a big question or I need some direction in my life, I drive out to Joshua Tree. This place always kills the noise right when you pull in. There is no phone reception. There are no buildings or houses. It's just wide-open wilderness. I'll fast, pray, and wander around the desert. I'll find myself a mound of rocks looking out over a view of the whole desert. I'll sit there and talk with God, maybe sing some worship songs that come to mind as I'm praying, and just wait for His voice. That day, His voice didn't come. That was very odd, because that had never happened to me before on one of my desert trips.

I started my drive back, thinking, "Well, I guess that's my answer. I told God that if He wanted me to have another kid, I needed to hear from Him. He didn't say anything—over and done. The end!" After three hours, I pulled into my driveway. Before going in, I said, "Okay, God, here's one last shot. I really need to hear from You if this is what You want. I'm going to walk into my house and go up to my daughters and ask them if they want a brother. If they are excited and say yes, then I'll take that as coming from You."

That probably won't seem like too high of a bar I set until

you get some background. First, we had never talked to our two-and-a-half-year-old daughters about a brother. I'm not even sure they knew what a brother was. And second, my daughters get thirty minutes of TV time before dinner. That's it—nothing more. So, when TV time comes, they are locked onto that screen. Our house could be burning down, and they'd never even notice the heat. I could ride in on a unicorn, do a backflip while blowing fire out of my mouth, and land in a pool of Jell-O and they wouldn't even look up. When I come home during TV time, I know that there is no chance I am going to be acknowledged until TV time is over and we're sitting down to eat. Believe me— I've tried many times with no luck. So, when I put this challenge out to God, I knew that it would take a miracle equivalent to the parting of the Red Sea to pull the girls' attention away from their show even just for a few seconds, let alone have them show any excitement about what I was saying.

I opened the front door and walked into the house. The triplets were sitting right where I knew they would be. They were totally glued to the show they were watching. I was thinking, "Awesome! I'm golden. There's no way I'm getting anything out of them." I said, "Hey, girls, what's up?" Nothing. No acknowledgment. Not even a head turn.

Here goes nothing. "Girls," I said. Still nothing. "Girls, do you want to have a baby brother?" All three turned toward me and screamed, "Yes!!" And inside I'm like, "Noooooo!! Are you kidding?" I was in shock—this was really happening. I thought it was a no-go for that whole three-hour drive home. I walked to Crystal in the kitchen, and I said, "All right, God finally spoke to me. Looks like we're going to have a baby boy." And when I said that to her, I got this bubbling spring of joy in my stomach.

It was one of the weirdest feelings I've ever had. It was the Holy Spirit confirming the words I had just spoken to Crystal. I don't think I'd ever had that feeling before, and I know I've never had it since. It was the most joy I have ever felt at one time. It was a supernatural affirmation that told me, "You finally stopped fighting it and said yes, Ryan. You're listening to Me now."

I really needed that affirmation. As I've already said, I had a list of reasons why I thought it wasn't a good idea. But I had also told God, "Not my will but Yours be done," and He took me up on my commitment. Then the joy came, and I was like, "Whoa! That was crazy!" In that moment my whole attitude changed. At the end of the day, I want whatever God thinks is best for me, so that's the way I live my life now. What He's leading me to do may not make sense at the time, but if it's His will, then I'll do it. It's simple, childlike faith.

Our God is a miracle-working God. When we couldn't have children, He gave us triplets. When the doctors said they couldn't survive the pregnancy, all three not only survived but are also healthy, growing, amazing girls. When He told Crystal through a prophetic word before she was even pregnant that He was going to give her a son, He ended up convincing me this was a good idea, too. He gave me joy about the whole decision, allowed her to get pregnant, and gave us the little boy He had promised her—born on my birthday of all days. When I look at this amazing child and see all the promise and potential in him, I realize that never have I been so thankful to have been so wrong.

The fact that God works miracles should give us hope. Hope

and peace that He is in control. Hope that He will carry us through whatever storm may come our way. God is in every detail of your life, because He loves you so much. You are so special to Him that He created you exactly as you are for such a time as this. As I said earlier, everyone in California is currently under a mandate from the governor to stay at home because of the coronavirus. It's still very early on and the president has just told America to expect two very difficult weeks. What are those weeks going to look like? I don't know. But I can tell you that I am at complete peace, because all I need to do is to look at my three girls and my son to be reminded that God has got this whole thing completely under control. He has a plan that He wants to carry out in each of our lives, and He can and will do whatever is necessary to do what is best for us.

Because of that confidence in God, I am looking forward. Too many people are paralyzed because of their fear. Others are saying, "We need to figure out what things are going to look like when this is all over before we can start planning for the future." Forget that! I'm still praying, "God, what are You going to do next? What can I be doing now to prepare for what You have next for me personally and for The Whosoevers Movement?" I'm living expecting God to work.

A few years ago someone shared with me a prophetic word that they had about The Whosoevers moving into a huge building and having all kinds of rad things going on inside—music, skating, art. It was all about having a creative compound. Since that time, a number of other people independent of each other have shared that same big-building vision with me. I'm expecting it to happen. I'm not chasing after it—that's not what you do with visions and dreams. You don't follow them; you pray and you make room in your life for God to make it happen. That's what I'm doing now. COVID-19 hasn't squashed that vision. God isn't in heaven saying, "Now I have to send a vision to someone so they can let Ryan know that because of the coronavirus the whole building thing is off." I'm praying, He's moving, and in His time that building project will come. Maybe you'll even get to read about it online after you finish this chapter!

God's got plans for us, and He is moving forward in the midst of this pandemic. Are you ready for Him to launch you? I wish I could tell you exactly how this is all going to play out, but I can't. However, even if somehow I get sick or die from this virus, I'm still good. Paul wrote, "If we live, it's to honor the Lord. And if we die, it's to honor the Lord. So whether we live or die, we belong to the Lord" (Romans 14:8). We have the certain hope that God is working out His best plan for us no matter what the outcome is. My mom is battling cancer right now. If He heals her or if He takes her to be with Him, she is good either way. Our God has the love to want what's best for us, the wisdom to know what is best for us, and the power to do what is best for us. Because of that, when we put our hope in Him, we will never be put to shame.

CHAPTER 10

No Posers

What if you're out skating a park and you see a dude show up? He has the new board, the shoes—the whole new kit from head to toe. He looks like he might be sponsored. As he's sitting and watching everyone skate, you notice his board with its sick graphic on the bottom. Next thing you know, he starts rubbing the nose and tail of the board back and forth on the curb where he's sitting. He gets up and walks to the rail and does the same on the bottom graphic, scuffing it so it looks like he's been shredding the park. Then he starts walking around the park—never skating, just walking.

He moves up to a ledge and stands there. You think, "What's this guy's deal?" Then, instead of skating, he pulls out his phone and starts posing for selfies. When he's done, he walks out of the park. Later, you're scanning your social media and you stumble across this dude's feed. In it, he's talking about how rad his time at the park was today. He's bragging to everyone that his session skating the ledge was so sick. What is the first word that would come to your mind? Exactly—poser!

A poser is someone who tries to look the part and talk the talk but doesn't have the passion or discipline to actually be who he's posing to be. You can find posers everywhere if you look closely enough. They're all over social media. They're all around high school and college campuses. You'll even find a lot of posers in church on Sunday. They're carrying their Bibles, singing the songs, dropping some cash in the plate. Shoot, they even quote verse after verse by memory when you're talking to them. But they're just going through the motions. They're not really living the life.

You're either the real deal or you're fake. Just a heads-up for some of you who may be new to following Jesus—watch out who you're attaching yourself to or hanging with. Just because they walk like a Christian and talk like a Christian and pray like a Christian and go to church like a Christian doesn't mean they are a Christian.

Or, maybe you're the one playing the Christian game. You're all peace and love and light on the outside, but inside you're filled with sin and darkness. Jesus said in Matthew 6, "Your eye is like a lamp that provides light for your body. When your eye is healthy, your whole body is filled with light. But when your eye is unhealthy, your whole body is filled with darkness. And if the light you think you have is actually darkness, how deep that darkness is!" (vv. 22–23). If that's you and you're not making any effort to live the Christ-centered life, then you need to step up your game. Jesus called out the Pharisees, the big-dog religious leaders of those days, for living this way, calling them "whitewashed tombs"—looking so fresh and so clean on the outside, while inside they were filled with stinky, rotten flesh and bones. Straight up death! Jesus is looking for those ready to pick up their cross, not those who only want to sit back and talk about the cross. He's looking for fully committed hearts of obedience and worship. What does your heart look like right now?

Jesus and His disciples were in Bethany hanging with His friends Lazarus, Mary, and Martha. He had first met this little family—two sisters and a brother—sometime before and had built a great relationship with them. "As Jesus and the disciples continued on their way to Jerusalem, they came to a certain village where a woman named Martha welcomed him into her home. Her sister, Mary, sat at the Lord's feet, listening to what he taught. But Martha was distracted by the big dinner she was preparing" (Luke 10:38–40). Check out Mary—she was connected in with Jesus, absorbing every word that He spoke. Martha was missing everything that Jesus said, because she was too worried about getting everything done. When Martha complained to Jesus that it wasn't fair—she was doing all the work while Mary was just kicking it in the living room—Jesus replied, "My dear Martha, you are worried and upset over all these details! There is only one thing worth being concerned about. Mary has discovered it, and it will not be taken away from her" (vv. 41–42).

We meet Lazarus a little later, after he's dead...and then he's not. More on that in a minute. But what we know about this family of siblings is that they all have great character and they all love Jesus. They just show it in different ways. Mary is the worshipper. Martha is the worker. Lazarus is the witness. All three are amazing, because they all just want to serve and follow Jesus.

Jesus and His crew were hanging out at the home of these three, and they were about to have some dinner. They had spent the past three or four hours walking toward Jerusalem. Bethany was two miles shy of the big city, so they had pulled up short there. They were hot, sweaty, dusty, and tired. Jesus knew that the next day was going to get crazy. It was going to start with Him revealing that He is the Messiah and the Son of God. He was going to ride into Jerusalem on a donkey, while all the people around Him would be waving palm branches and crying out, "Hosanna, hosanna! Blessed is He who comes in the name of the Lord!" Then He had to make a stop at the Temple, where He was going to tear it up again like He had done at the beginning of His ministry. The rest of the day would be spent teaching the crowds, battling with the religious leaders, and healing anyone who came His way. So tonight, Jesus just wanted to kick back with His crew.

The disciple John, who was there for the meal, wrote, "A dinner was prepared in Jesus' honor. Martha served, and Lazarus was among those who ate with him" (John 12:2). Martha, true to her character, was serving Jesus. She was like, "Come on, boys, we've got the best hummus in town. And the pita bread? C'mon now...let's get this party started." Notice that John made sure that all the future readers of his Gospel knew that Lazarus was there eating with the rest of them. He was making a point here. There were those who doubted that Lazarus was actually alive. But John was saying, "Hey, if any of you were thinking that this was some kind of *Weekend at Bernie's* thing where they propped Lazarus up at the table, think again. He was actually eating and breathing."

Imagine what it would have been like to have been there just listening. I can't help but picture it as if it were me and my friends getting together. It could have gone down like this. The disciples would probably say, "Hey, what's going on, Mary, Martha? Lazarus, what's up? It's been a minute since we last saw you." Lazarus shoots back, "Not much, man. What about you guys?"

Andrew says, "You know the Pharisees have been after us, so we've been hanging out in Ephraim."

Lazarus laughs. "You mean the village in the wilderness? Dude, not much going on out there."

"Tell me about it," says Matthew. "Nothing but dirt and rocks and snakes and spiders—"

"And scorpions," interrupts John. "Ask Matthew about when I put that snake in his tent. He screamed like a little girl. That was classic."

Everyone busts up laughing. Matthew says, "Dude, snakes are sketchy."

James looks back at Lazarus and says, "So, seriously, man, what's up with you? Last time we saw you, you had died. That had to be weird. Are people still tripping on you being back alive and all?"

"Dude, people keep coming by the house from all over the place just to check me out—see if I really am alive. It's crazy. The word is out. I went viral overnight. I've got to start selling tickets or something."

By that time, everyone is dipping the bread in the sauce and chasing it with some lamb kebabs. Jesus is busting up laughing, but He's still holding a little back. He knows He's heading to the cross, so He's got a lot on His mind.

Peter looks at Jesus and says, "Yeah, Jesus, You got the word and You were like, 'So, my man Lazarus is really sick, but we're going to hang around here long enough for him to die and sit in the grave for a few days. Then we'll cruise on over so I can bring him back to life.'"

They all bust up laughing. Lazarus loses it and shoots the drink out of his nose. "Seriously?" he asks, after wiping his mouth and catching his breath. "You never told me that part. Dude, that's messed up!"

Jesus just shrugs His shoulders with a grin, throws a thumb at Lazarus, and says, "This guy…"

Matthew points at Thomas the scaredy-cat and says, "He was saying, 'Yeah, great idea going back to Jerusalem. They wanted to stone us to death last time. So why don't we all go back and die together?'" Thomas opens his mouth to defend himself but shuts it again because he can't.

Peter picks the story back up. "We get here and Jesus says, 'Roll the stone aside,' and everyone started freaking out! 'No way! Dude's going to stink by now! What are You doing, Jesus?'" Even Jesus had to laugh at that one.

Then Jesus picks up the narrative from Peter. "I just tell them again, 'Pull it aside.' They do. Then I pray, 'God, because You always hear Me, I'm doing this for the benefit of the people around Me. Lazarus, come out!' And out came the walking mummy."

I don't know. It could have happened like that. Just some

good times, kicking back around a table, telling stories, making fun of each other—doing what friends do. I don't picture them just sitting there all holy and subdued with little golden halos around their heads. But then in came Mary and everything changed.

———————

The conversation was going on, and then in came Mary the worshipper. Seems we always tend to find Mary at the feet of Jesus. This is no exception. "Then Mary took a twelve-ounce jar of expensive perfume made from essence of nard, and she anointed Jesus' feet with it, wiping his feet with her hair. The house was filled with the fragrance" (John 12:3). Picture a jar the size of a soda can filled with that stuff. She rolled around the table and sat at Christ's feet. She opened the jar and started pouring— anointing Jesus' head and His feet.

Then she did something that is amazing. She let down her hair—something Jewish women would never do in public— and began wiping His feet with her hair. That's like the ultimate in humility, doubled. First the hair came down; then it went to Jesus' feet. Seriously, talk about nasty. I don't like feet—period. But dirty feet? That's nasty. People of that time walked everywhere in their sandals, which means they all had mud-caked, sewage-soaked, callous-toed feet. Jesus included. His were like everybody else's. Yet here was Mary, wiping them with her hair. Can you imagine what she looked like after she was done—face streaked from her tears and her hair crusty from the mud?

But Mary didn't care. She was in tune, living out James 4:10: "Humble yourselves before the Lord, and he will lift you up in honor." Because she worshipped at Jesus' feet, she was ready for when God wanted to use her to prepare Jesus for the most important event in history—His death on the cross. And because she humbled herself, she is honored—by God and by us two thousand years later who are still talking about how amazing she is for doing what she did.

Why do I say that the cross is the most important event in history? It's because all of our hope is put in what Jesus did when He was crucified. Jesus said,

> No one has ever gone to heaven and returned. But the Son of Man has come down from heaven. And as Moses lifted up the bronze snake on a pole in the wilderness, so the Son of Man must be lifted up, so that everyone who believes in him will have eternal life. For this is how God loved the world: He gave his one and only Son, so that everyone who believes in him will not perish but have eternal life. (John 3:13–16)

Everything you need to know about eternal life is right in those words from John 3. Jesus was raised up on a cross. That passage says that if you believe that by Him dying and being raised up on the third day you can receive forgiveness and life, you will be saved. Being "saved" just means that you will not go to hell. That's what Jesus meant by "will not perish."

Jesus went on to say, "God sent his Son into the world not to judge the world, but to save the world through him" (John 3:17). Jesus didn't come to judge you for your sin. He came to give you a way out. He came to forgive you, not to bring you punishment. He wants to save you right here, right now, even as you are reading this book. Whatever mountains are in your way, whatever issues you are going through, whatever sins are dragging you down, God will be there for you. You just need to believe by faith, and He will save you.

Mary the worshipper is there at Jesus' feet, and she is doing things right. But she's not the only person around the dinner table. "Judas Iscariot, the disciple who would soon betray him, said, 'That perfume was worth a year's wages'" (John 12:4–5). Judas the betrayer—total contrast to Mary the worshipper. Mary is busy honoring God with a super expensive gift. Judas is worried about the cash. Mary is wondering how she can sacrifice and give more. Judas is plotting out how he can skim a little of the sacrifice into his own pocket. I don't know for sure how much a year's wages was back then. Today, I guess it just depends on your job. You could be making anywhere from $20K to $120K. Any way you look at it, that was some expensive perfume she was pouring out on Jesus' feet, and Judas was having none of it. "'It should have been sold and the money given to the poor.' Not that he cared for the poor—he was a thief, and since he was in charge of the disciples' money, he often stole some for himself" (vv. 5–6).

So, here's Judas posing as a good Christian, because "Christian" just means a follower of Jesus Christ. He's trying to make it look like he's spiritual and cares about the poor. "Oh, Mary, what are you doing? We could have taken that and sold it and fed the hungry children. We could have adopted a homeless child or given it to some clean water initiative. But instead you just wasted it on Jesus' feet." I'm sure that some of the disciples were agreeing with him, because his logic was sound. It's a good thing to feed the poor. We should all help out those who are needy. This just wasn't that time. Ecclesiastes 3 says that there is a time for everything. This wasn't the time for feeding the poor; this was the time for preparing Jesus to go to the cross. Mary knew that because she was in tune with Christ. Judas was clueless, because he was only out for himself. He was a man who followed his flesh and body appetites. He didn't care about the poor. Dude was a snake, a crook. He was a liar, a thief, and a betrayer. With a character like that, his heart was far from God. There's no way he could have had any clue what God was doing.

If you say you skateboard but you don't, then you're a poser. Guys who say they play guitar, and even post pictures of themselves on their social media jamming, but in real life don't play a thing, they're posers, too. In the same way, there are poser Christians—frauds, wannabes, hypocrites. They give real Christians a bad name because they're fake. That was Judas.

This guy had been with Jesus for three years. Undoubtedly, in that time he had heard some of the gnarliest Bible studies of all time from Him. He'd seen Jesus heal people, cast out demons, feed the five thousand. He was in the boat when Jesus told the storm to stop. On his watch, Jesus made the deaf hear and the blind see. He even raised the dead—the evidence of which was sitting right there at the same table with him. Yet all of this made no impact on his life—there was no transformation that took place. That is scary. How blind was this guy?

The thing is Judas had everyone around him—except Jesus—totally fooled. All the disciples were thinking that he was completely legit. But he wasn't legit. He was a poser, and a really good one at that. How many people in the church today are just like Judas? How many come to Bible study week after week, they're at every Sunday service, they're dropping their cash in the offering, they're going to the men's and women's conferences, they're going through all the motions but there is nothing real there? They are connected to the church, but they're not connected to Jesus. There has been no transformation in their lives. They are still men and women of the flesh—whitewashed tombs like Jesus called the Pharisees.

If you have given your life to Christ and you call yourself a Christian, then you should be progressing and growing for the better. If you are not manifesting the fruit of the Spirit, then you better take a second look. Don't waste any more time. I'm not judging your salvation, but I am suggesting you do some serious evaluation to see if your commitment was actually real. Jesus' brother James wrote, "Now someone may argue, 'Some people have faith; others have good deeds.' But I say, 'How can you show me your faith if you don't have good deeds? I will show you my faith by my good deeds'" (James 2:18). What he's saying is that if you can't point to ways you are drawing closer to Christ and serving Him, you need to check yourself to make sure you're not just a poser. Have you really made Jesus the center of your life, or are you just playing the game? Because "playing the game" is one of the paths that the devil has laid out to lead us down to hell.

Jesus said, "You can enter God's Kingdom only through the narrow gate. The highway to hell is broad, and its gate is wide for the many who choose that way. But the gateway to life is very narrow and the road is difficult, and only a few ever find it" (Matthew 7:13–14). Why is the way to hell broad and full of people? Because it holds a billion different ways to get there. One of the wider lanes on that road is playing the fake disciple while you follow your own way. Notice that Jesus said that many choose that way. Nobody forces you onto the poser path. It's something you choose.

The path to life, however, is narrow. Why is it so difficult to get to heaven? Jesus said this: "If any of you wants to be my follower, you must give up your own way" (Matthew 16:24). What is our own way? It's those body appetites—lying, cheating, betraying, sleeping around, drugs, anger, bitterness. He goes on to say, "[You must] take up your cross, and follow me. If you try to hang on to your life, you will lose it. But if you give up your life for my sake, you will save it. And what do you benefit if you gain the whole world but lose your own soul? Is anything worth more than your soul?" (vv. 24–26). Judas wasn't ready for that type of commitment. While the rest of the disciples were giving up their lives, Judas was busy giving up his soul. Are you selling your soul for anything? Is there anything in your life that you are putting before God? If you are, is it really worth it? Does it really make sense to you to give up eternity? Making a decision on eternity is like buying a house. You ask any Realtor, and they'll tell you it's all about location, location, location. What location do you want for your eternity—heaven with its peace and love or hell with its fire and torment?

Back to the narrow road in Matthew 7. Jesus was about to drop the hammer on the posers. He said, "Not everyone who calls out to me, 'Lord! Lord!' will enter the Kingdom of Heaven" (v. 21a). He was saying, "Not everyone who prays a prayer and says, 'Jesus, forgive me for my sins' is a Christian. Not everyone who goes to church on Sundays is a Christian." Why not? Because heaven's doors are not opened by saying some magic words or by meeting in some building once a week. Instead, Jesus said, "Only those who actually do the will of my Father in heaven will enter" (v. 21b). No posers. No wannabes. Only those who truly follow God. Hear me clearly—it's not doing good things that will get you into heaven. Doing God's will is proof that He has already forgiven you and given you eternal life.

Jesus continued: "On judgment day many will say to me, 'Lord! Lord! We prophesied in your name and cast out demons in your name and performed many miracles in your name.' But I will reply, 'I never knew you. Get away from me, you who break God's laws'" (vv. 22–23). What's this judgment day He is talking about? In Revelation 20, we read about a great white throne that God Himself will sit on. From that position, He will judge every person based on whether or not they trusted in Jesus to forgive their sins. If they did and they made Him the Lord of their life, then their name was written in the Book of Life. If they didn't, it wouldn't have been. There are major consequences for not having your name written in that book. "Anyone whose name was not found recorded in the Book of Life was thrown into the lake of fire" (v. 15). That lake of fire is hell. So many of those people will be ones who heard the truth about Jesus their whole lives but never acted on it.

Jesus said that only those who do His Father's will can expect their name to be in that book. Why? Again, it's because living the way God has called you to live is evidence that you truly gave your whole life to Him. If you are a 100 percent skateboarder and not a poser, then you look like a skater, talk and act like one, read the skate magazines, watch the videos, and know the difference between regular- and switch-stance tricks—and you actually skate! If we don't want to be fake Christians, then we have to read the Bible, learn what Jesus says to do, and then do it.

Back at the dinner table with Mary and the boys, Jesus put Judas on blast: "Leave her alone. She did this in preparation for my burial. You will always have the poor among you, but you will not always have me" (John 12:7–8). Judas didn't like getting the smackdown treatment. It would be just a few days later that he would be with the religious leaders, selling Jesus out. "Thirty pieces of silver, and I'll show you right where you can snatch Him up." A lot of people don't like being called out for how they are just doing church. "Who are you to tell me how to be a Christian? My faith is between me and my God." First off, I'm not calling you out for anything. I'm just telling you what the Bible says. Don't listen to my words; listen to Jesus' words. Look at what the Bible teaches. The Bible is a mirror—when you read it, you will see what you look like. And when you see who you are, you need to do something about it. The Bible says,

> For if you listen to the word and don't obey, it is like glancing at your face in a mirror. You see yourself, walk away, and forget what you look like. But if you look carefully into the perfect law that sets you free, and if you do what it says and don't forget what you heard, then God will bless you for doing it. (James 1:23–25)

The Word of God is what exposes us for being posers—hearers and not doers. That is why I read the Bible—I want to know what needs to change. And when God shows me what to change, I don't just walk away and forget what I look like. I change it. That's what will keep me from ever becoming a poser, because being a poser is the worst thing ever.

Where do you stand? We've all got to analyze our lives. Are we like Judas, posing like we're someone we're not? It's time, guys. God loves you to death—to death on the cross two thousand years ago when He died for the sins of humankind. He has a plan for you. He wants to fill you with His Holy Spirit—with fire and power. He wants to make you a true disciple like Mary.

To be a Mary—a true worshipper—we have to read the Bible. We have to pray. We have to listen to what is being said; then we have to apply it to our lives. That's when God can use us for the important things He has planned for us.

Jesus is coming. The King is coming. Our job is just like that of John the Baptist. He prepared the nation of Israel for the coming Messiah. We have that same Great Commission. We are called to point the way to Jesus. We are commissioned to preach and teach and live the words of salvation. Remember, salvation is the good news of the Gospel message.

It starts when we repent of our sins so that we can be forgiven through Jesus dying on the cross for us. That's what opens the door to eternal life. That's when the Holy Spirit comes into you, fills you up, and gives you an amazing peace. The Spirit also gives you a fire—a passion to serve your Lord and Savior. He's got that passion ready for you if you'll just open yourself to Him. He wants to do a work in you so that He can do a work through you. When you are filled with the Holy Spirit, torrents of living water will pour into you. That's when you'll start seeing God working the supernatural in this natural world.

Dude, that is my life every day. It's not like I get up every morning and pray, "Okay, God, let's do this. I want to see some signs and wonders!" I just make myself ready for what He wants to do. It starts with reading the Bible. It's through prayer and reading the Scriptures that we'll hear His voice. Then He'll just bring people in front of me. I'll be sitting in a restaurant, and some dude will sit across from me. In my mind I'll be thinking, "Come on, God, I don't want to pray for this guy right now. I'm hungry. I just want to eat my tacos." But then the guy will say, "Man, I was suicidal…" And suddenly, I find myself forgetting about my tacos and drawn into serving God by loving this guy. That's what real life is. It's loving God and loving people. It's saying, "God, I just want to be used by You." Then He'll bring people to you, and you'll start leading them to the Lord and praying for them, and you may even see people getting healed.

That's the Mary life. Stop the Judas poser life. It didn't end well for him, just like it doesn't end well for anyone else. But if you go all in for Christ, fully committed, you'll have a life of passion and purpose as you fill your role in carrying out the Great Commission. So decide today: Who are you going to be? Will you be Mary the worshipper—Spirit-led and in tune with God? Or are you going to be Judas the big poser—a white-washed tomb, stinking like dead bodies?

We're at the end and it's decision time. You may be saying, "Okay, man, I want to be fully committed. What do I do? I'm tired of being tired. I want to have peace and joy. I want to live the life that God created me for. I want Him to use my life."

It's so simple. You just need to open your heart and talk to

God. No games—you just get real with Him. Say, "Jesus, forgive me of all my sins. I'm a sinner, but I am repenting now. Fill me with Your Holy Spirit and use my life for Your glory from this day on. I am all in—one hundred percent!"

Now your name is written in the Book of Life. You are sealed and set for heaven. Get busy serving God. Use the time He's given you on this earth to make a difference. This is where it all begins. This is your Panama City hotel room moment. That one day changed my life and led me to become the man I am today. Just think what God can do in and through you if you will simply put the past behind and "press on to reach the end of the race and receive the heavenly prize for which God, through Christ Jesus, is calling [you]" (Philippians 3:14).

ACKNOWLEDGMENTS

God rules! All praise to the Father, the Son, and the Holy Spirit.

Thank you to my parents, Raul and Sharon Ries, and to the rest of my family, relatives, and friends for all of your prayers and support, and for believing in me. I love you all very much, and I'm very grateful for you.

Shout out to Sonny Sandoval of P.O.D., Brian Welch of Korn, Lacey Sturm, Dale Goddard, Sean McKeehan, Cathy Barrett, Wade O'Neill, Nick Melendrez, Michael Guido, and Calvary Chapel Golden Springs for coming together in unity to birth the Whosoevers Movement, and thanks to all the Whosoevers staff from the beginning until now for your hard work, blood, sweat, and years.

I want to give a big thanks to my writing partner, Steve Yohn—an incredibly gifted writer who helped me make this book happen.

Thank you to my father and Chuck Smith (founder of the Calvary Chapel Movement) for teaching me how to study and understand the Bible, for training me to teach the Word myself, and for demonstrating to me how to operate and move in the Holy Spirit. Thanks also to all the other pastors—you know who you are—who have taken the time to pour into me, and who gave me a chance when I first started. This gratitude also goes out to the many other churches and ministry partners we have worked with that have helped take The Whosoevers Movement around the world. Thanks to Angie Clawson and the I Am Second team. Much love to all the radio stations across the country that have picked up *The Ryan Ries Show* and gotten behind The Whosoevers Movement. And a huge thank you to all the Whosoevers around the world who have supported us with your love and prayers.

Massive thanks to JW Clarke of Birdhouse and the Billy Graham Evangelistic Association for setting up the meeting with Yates & Yates that ultimately birthed this whole project. Thanks to Matt Yates for your wisdom and expertise through this process. Finally, thanks to Beth Adams, my editor; Daisy Hutton, my publisher; and the whole team at Worthy.

NOTES

1   Dennis Thompson, "Study Sees Link between Porn and Sexual Dysfunction," WebMD, May 12, 2017, https://www.webmd.com/sex/news/20170512/study-sees-link-between-porn-and-sexual-dysfunction#1.

2   Norman Doidge, "Brain Scans of Porn Addicts: What's Wrong with This Picture?," *The Guardian*, September 26, 2013, https://www.theguardian.com/commentisfree/2013/sep/26/brain-scans-porn-addicts-sexual-tastes.

3   "Age of First Exposure to Pornography Shapes Men's Attitudes toward Women," American Psychological Association, August 3, 2017, https://www.apa.org/news/press/releases/2017/08/pornography-exposure.

4   Chuck Smith, "Why Grace Changes Everything," November 21, 2003. https://www.cclakeside.com/wp-content/uploads/2017/04/Why-Grace-Changes-Everything.pdf.

5   "Child Abuse Statistics," Ark of Hope for Children, April 9, 2019, https://www.arkofhopeforchildren.org/child-abuse/child-abuse-statistics-info.

6   "Definition of Sin," Harvest, accessed August 4, 2020, https://harvest.org/know-god-article/definition-of-sin/.

7   Chuck Smith, *Living Water: The Power of the Holy Spirit in Your Life* (Word for Today, 2007).

8   Brian Broderson. "Chuck Smith's Vision for the Future of the Calvary Chapel Movement," Calvary Chapel, September 1, 2014. https://calvarychapel.com/posts/chuck-smiths-vision-for-the-future-of-the-calvary-chapel-movement.

ABOUT THE AUTHOR

RYAN RIES is the co-founder of The Whosoevers Movement, an evangelistic outreach to people around the world. Ryan hosts *The Ryan Ries Show*, a podcast and nationwide radio show heard on more than 114 radio stations, and he speaks regularly at Calvary Chapel Golden Springs in Diamond Bar, California, where his messages air on FM radio around the world. Ryan speaks about 250 times a year and has shared messages of hope and salvation to hundreds of thousands of people at music festivals, schools, and churches around the globe. His testimony film by I Am Second has reached hundreds of thousands of viewers worldwide.

For ten years, Ries was the director of skate and music marketing for internationally known brands, including C1RCA Footwear, Special Blend, and Foursquare Outerwear. In 2000, he managed one of the top skateboard teams in the world, and with a network of friends, helped bring the underground skate and music scene together to create Skate Jam 2000, the first and largest festival-style contest of its kind. For many years, worldly success and pleasure defined Ryan's life until a near cocaine overdose caught his attention, and he surrendered his life to the Lord. Following his conversion, Ries gave up the addictions that once consumed him and now spends his life speaking to students worldwide, helping them break free from addiction and leading them to Christ.

Ryan lives in Southern California with his wife, Crystal, their triplet daughters, and baby son.

For more on Ryan, go to www.Ryan-Ries.com.

THE
RYAN
RIES
SHOW
SAT NIGHTS 9PM
WATCH ON THE WHOSOEVERS APP
or RYANRIES.COM
THE WHOSOEVERS
LEADING THE WAY TO REFLECT
CHRIST IN CULTURE
THEWHOSOEVERS.COM
@thewhosoevers

IAMSECOND.COM/RYAN-RIES

I AM SECOND